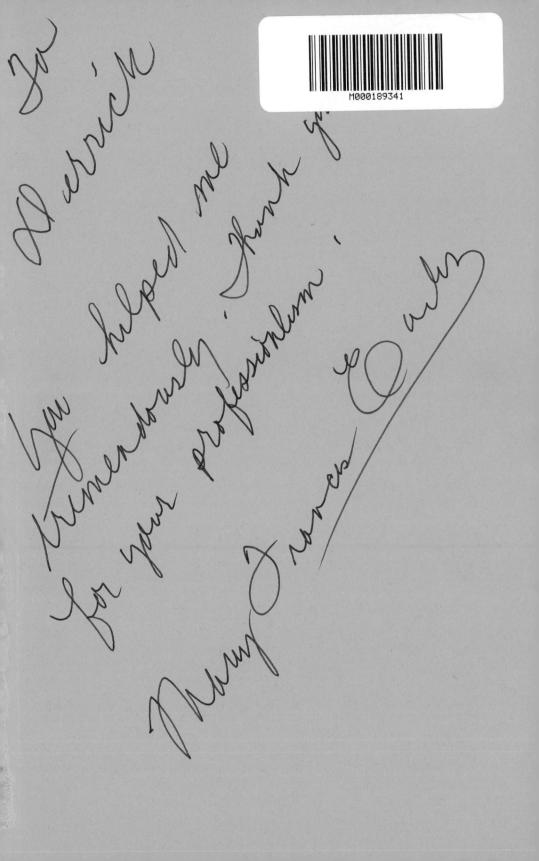

To
Derrick,

You helped me
tremendously. Thank you
for your professionalism.

Mary Travers Curtis

The Quiet Trailblazer

My Journey as the First Black Graduate of the University of Georgia

MARY FRANCES EARLY

Published by the Mary Frances Early College of Education
and the University of Georgia Libraries
Athens

Published by the Mary Frances Early College of Education
and the University of Georgia Libraries

Distributed by the University of Georgia Press
Athens, Georgia 30602
www.ugapress.org

Printed and bound by Integrated Books International

The paper in this book meets the guidelines for
permanence and durability of the Committee on
Production Guidelines for Book Longevity of the
Council on Library Resources.

Printed in the United States of America
21 22 23 24 25 C 5 4 3 2 1

ISBN 978-0-8203-6081-2 (hardcover)
ISBN 978-0-8203-6082-9 (ebook)

To my parents,

John Henry Early

&

Annie Ruth Early,

who gave me roots to ground me

in my rich legacy and

wings to propel me

to the zenith of my abilities

No one can make you feel inferior without your consent.

—ELEANOR ROOSEVELT

Contents

———

Foreword

Dr. Maurice Daniels

———————

Dr. Carter G. Woodson observed, "Those who have no record of what their forebears have accomplished lose the inspiration which comes from the teaching of biography and history." This memoir presents the deeply inspiring story of Mary Frances Early, tracing her journey as a courageous trailblazer in the struggle for social justice. On August 16, 1962, Early became the first Black graduate of the University of Georgia (UGA) and the first Black graduate of any of the so-called white public colleges and universities in the University System of Georgia. She is rightly revered today by all those who believe in the cause of social justice.

In 1997, while researching a book and public television documentary chronicling the story of Horace T. Ward, I was privileged to interview many courageous lawyers and other leaders whose work was pivotal in achieving the U.S. Supreme Court victory that led to the desegregation of UGA.[1] They included legendary attorney Donald Lee Hollowell, Georgia's chief civil rights lawyer during the 1950s and 1960s; prominent businessman and civil rights activist Jesse Hill; the bold and courageous Constance Baker Motley, who was the first Black woman to serve on the federal bench; and the eminent civil rights leader Vernon E. Jordan.

Through these interviews I learned of Mary Frances Early, a little-known but significant figure in the desegregation of UGA. Vernon Jordan said of Early in his interview, "She came as a graduate student to the university, did very well, and was actually the first Black to earn a degree because she got her master's degree before Hamp [Hamilton Holmes] and Charlayne [Hunter] were able to finish." Jordan opined, "But she is a pioneer too! She was not involved in the lawsuit and therefore did not share in the celebrity. That makes her no less of a celebrity in my judgment."[2]

Yet despite her historic achievement as the first African American graduate of UGA, Early had been largely overlooked by scholarly histories, omitted from media reports chronicling the Black freedom struggle, and even ignored by UGA itself. On the rare occasions when her story was mentioned, it was typically a mere footnote. Though I am deeply humbled and a bit embarrassed that Early repeatedly refers to me as her "discoverer," it was Jesse Hill and Donald Hollowell who urged me to interview Early and include her in my documentary on Horace T. Ward.

I was privileged to interview Early on February 19, 1997. She displayed a deep humility and modesty as she shared poignant stories about her loving and supportive family, her childhood in segregated Atlanta, her passion for education and stellar career in music education, and her commitment to the civil rights cause. In this deeply moving interview, Early also reflected on her struggle for admission to UGA, which her memoir discusses in great detail. Early shared that despite being UGA's first African American graduate, she had never been recognized or acknowledged by the university in the thirty-five years since her graduation. Though painfully disappointed that UGA had snubbed her for more than three decades, she graciously insisted that she harbored no ill will toward the university.

Early was featured in my 2000 public television documentary, Foot Soldier for Equal Justice: Horace T. Ward and the Struggle to Enter the University of Georgia.[3] In February 2000, Early accepted my invitation to attend the premiere of Part 1 of the documentary, which was held at UGA. It was a very special and historic event. On that February evening, Early was recognized for the very first time among her fellow trailblazers in UGA's desegregation history. Other distinguished pioneers attending the premiere included Donald Hollowell, federal judge Horace Ward, civil rights activist Rev. Archibald Killian, and the illustrious families of the late Dr. Hamilton Holmes and the late Dr. William Madison Boyd.[4]

UGA doctoral students Tracey Ford and Valerie White, who helped produce the documentary, had learned the details of Early's role as UGA's first Black graduate as they helped in the film production. Ford and White were deeply moved and inspired by Early's untold story. Shortly after the premiere, they approached me about inviting her back to campus to speak to the Graduate and Professional Scholars (GAPS) organization.

Ford and White were members of GAPS, a group comprised predominantly of African American graduate and professional students that focused on the recruitment and retention of historically underrepresented students. I served as co-adviser of GAPS with UGA staff member B. Lynne Reeder. Led by President Jessica DeCuir, GAPS unanimously supported inviting Early to speak and approved a resolution to establish an annual lecture series named in her honor.

Early returned to campus on April 18, 2000, to deliver the inaugural Mary Frances Early Lecture. Prior to the lecture, Meg Amstutz, assistant to UGA president Michael Adams, presented a historic proclamation on behalf of the president formally recognizing Early as UGA's first African American graduate. Early then delivered a powerful and inspiring lecture.

Ford, White, DeCuir, and GAPS as a whole played a key role in helping illuminate Early's enormous contributions to UGA, celebrating her legacy at the annual lecture, and pushing UGA to recognize her more prominently. Ford, White, and DeCuir all went on to earn PhDs from UGA, inspired in large measure by Early's example of determination and perseverance. During my service as GAPS co-adviser, numerous GAPS students credited Early with inspiring them to persist in earning graduate and professional degrees.

The Quiet Trailblazer is a gracefully written, eye-opening firsthand account of Mary Frances Early's story and her contributions to the Black freedom struggle. The book captures the authentic voice of an unsung grassroots activist who joined the civil rights movement to help defeat the ravages of Jim Crow in her home state. In so doing, she laid significant groundwork that helped change the course of history at UGA, in our state, and across the nation. The narrative brings to light the determination and grit of a native-born Georgia citizen who overcame layer upon layer of white supremacy to make history as the first African American to graduate from a university that had stubbornly maintained segregation for over 175 years.

The Quiet Trailblazer also recounts the distinguished honors UGA has bestowed on Early since her return to campus in 2000. In 2011, at the fiftieth anniversary celebration of the desegregation of UGA, Early was commemorated as a pioneer in UGA's desegregation alongside civil rights icons Hamilton Holmes and Charlayne Hunter, helping illuminate her previously untold story. Professor Derrick Alridge and Professor Cheryl Dozier, who co-chaired the event, advocated for honoring Early on this occasion. Subsequent distinctions include an honorary doctor of laws degree conferred by President Adams in 2013; the prestigious President's Medal presented by President Jere Morehead in 2018; and the renaming of the College of Education as the Mary Frances Early College of Education, approved by the Board of Regents in 2019.

In 2018, in collaboration with students and colleagues including co-executive producer Michelle Garfield Cook, I was honored to produce the public television documentary *Mary Frances Early: The Quiet Trailblazer*.[5] The documentary chronicles Early's upbringing in Atlanta; her struggle, sacrifice, and triumph as a central figure in desegregating UGA; and her brilliant and pioneering educational career. Narrated by esteemed journalist Monica Pearson, the documentary has aired on Georgia Public Broadcasting numerous times, offering a glimpse into Early's enduring legacy. In this book, however, Early provides us with the first full and comprehensive view of her compelling story.

Early embodies the unsung American hero in the struggle for equal justice. The recovery of hidden figures such as Early highlights the pivotal roles played by countless individuals, groups, and communities whose collective efforts produced sweeping social change.[6] Though well-known civil rights leaders such as Dr. Martin Luther King Jr., Rosa Parks, and Thurgood Marshall are rightly celebrated and have dominated the history of the civil rights movement, lesser-known activists such as Early also played a vital role in advancing the cause of social justice.

Civil rights scholarship has broadened its scope from chronicling primarily the narratives of nationally renowned figures to also illuminating the stories of the movement's lesser-known foot soldiers.[7] Historian Evelyn Brooks Higginbotham points out that it was not until the mid-1980s that local movement scholars began to look more closely at grassroots activism, which led to the discovery of previously unknown men and women in the Black freedom struggle.[8] Higginbotham notes, "Their attention to grassroots activism has facilitated important new work on Black women's roles in the movement."[9] This new work on the story of Mary Frances Early makes a significant contribution to this literature. Recognizing this unheralded freedom fighter enhances our appreciation of the struggles faced by ordinary citizens who accomplish extraordinary things.

The Quiet Trailblazer demonstrates how Early influenced social change from the ground up within the broader civil rights movement. Illuminating Early's story helps us achieve a more accurate and comprehensive understanding of the civil rights struggle. The narrative captures her civil rights work as well as the work of grassroots leaders such as Jesse Hill and Donald Hollowell, who helped her gain admission to UGA and supported her as she confronted daunting challenges at the university in 1961 and 1962. Her story explores the solidarity of the Black community in the struggle to open UGA to Black students and the courage of white allies who stepped up to support Early as she faced resistance and turmoil at UGA.

This book captures Early's enormous contributions to the campaign for racial equality in Georgia, contributions made with tremendous grace and dignity and incredible humility. Early's courageous and tenacious efforts helped build the foundation to defeat Jim Crow in Georgia's public colleges and universities, ultimately helping to transform the South. Early is one of the founders of a new UGA, a new Georgia, and a new South that make real the promise of democracy. She helped bring to life the Jeffersonian ideal, "We hold these truths to be self-evident, that all men [and women] are created equal, that they are endowed by their

Creator with certain unalienable Rights, that among these are Life, Liberty and the pursuit of Happiness." Each of us owes a debt of gratitude to Mary Frances: for her courage, her pioneering achievements, and her brilliant and stirring narrative.

NOTES

1. *Holmes v. Danner*, 195 F. Supp. 394 (M. D. Ga. 1961); Maurice C. Daniels, *Horace T. Ward: Desegregation of the University of Georgia, Civil Rights Advocacy, and Jurisprudence* (Atlanta: Clark Atlanta University Press, 2001).

2. Vernon E. Jordan Jr., interview with Maurice C. Daniels, February 28, 1997, Atlanta, Georgia.

3. *Foot Soldier for Equal Justice: Horace T. Ward and the Desegregation of the University of Georgia*, Maurice C. Daniels, executive producer; Janice Reaves, producer; George Rodrigues, co-producer; Derrick P. Alridge, academic adviser. Georgia Public Television Broadcast. Athens: University of Georgia Center for Continuing Education, 2000.

4. Dr. William Madison Boyd, Atlanta University professor and president of the Georgia NAACP, coalesced with Thurgood Marshall and the NAACP to dismantle segregation in Georgia's public colleges and universities and was the key adviser to Horace T. Ward in his efforts to enter the UGA School of Law. The family of civil rights activist Archibald Killian housed Hamilton Holmes during his enrollment at UGA. The Killian home and restaurant were places of refuge for Holmes, Charlayne Hunter, and Early during their journey at UGA.

5. *Mary Frances Early: The Quiet Trailblazer*, Maurice C. Daniels, executive producer; Michelle Garfield Cook, co-executive producer; Bobby Mitchell, editor; Greg Morrison, LaGeris Underwood Bell, Janice Reaves, producers. Georgia Public Television Broadcast, Athens: Foot Soldier Project for Civil Rights Studies, 2018.

6. Maurice C. Daniels, *Saving the Soul of Georgia: Donald L. Hollowell and the Struggle for Civil Rights* (Athens: University of Georgia Press, 2013), 8.

7. Tomiko Brown-Nagin, *Courage to Dissent: Atlanta and the Long History of the Civil Rights Movement* (New York: Oxford University Press, 2011); Emilye Crosby, *Civil Rights History from the Ground Up: Local Struggles, a National Movement* (Athens: University of Georgia Press, 2012).

8. Evelyn Brooks Higginbotham, Foreword, in Jeanne Theoharis and Komozi Woodard (Eds.), *Freedom North: Black Freedom Struggles outside the South, 1940–1980* (New York: Palgrave Macmillan, 2003), ix.

9. Ibid.

Acknowledgments

Kudos to my developmental editor, Melissa Tufts. She led me through the editing process with patience, talent, and marvelous insight.

Many thanks to my friends Emmie and Johnny Lee who allowed me to begin serious writing at their splendid cabin in the lovely Blue Ridge mountains. Thanks, too, to my friend Yolanda Lewellyn who drove me to Blue Ridge and allowed me quiet time for reflection and writing.

I owe a debt of thanks also to my family and many friends who encouraged me to stay the course and complete my memoir.

And what a relief it was to have wonderful prepared meals brought to me when I really didn't have the time to cook! Thanks, Nancy Shealy and Tiffany Hutchins.

I will always be grateful to President Jere Morehead for his support and encouragement to pen this memoir as part of UGA's desegregation history.

Sincere thanks, also, to Monica Kaufman Pearson, Maurice Daniels, Hank Klibanoff, Derrick Alridge, and Charlayne Hunter-Gault who read my manuscript and gave valuable suggestions for improvement.

Deep appreciation to Lonnie King (deceased) and Rosa Hadley-Rice who helped me with details about our time as students at E. P. Johnson Elementary School.

And to those who assisted me in so many ways with transportation, purchasing groceries and other needed items, and trips to appointments, I cannot thank you enough. They include Joan Zion, Brenda Zion, Yolanda Lewellyn, Cynthia Terry, Candace Haynes, Donata Defilippi, Angela Birkes, Amy Widener, George Jarman, Patrice Hector, Sandra Kaye Locklin, Greg Morrison, William Garner and any others whom I may have forgotten. I could not have completed this story of my life's journey without your loyal help.

THE QUIET TRAILBLAZER

Prologue

W hen one takes a walk down memory lane, many reflections evoke a sense of nostalgia. Some memories represent joyful or halcyon times that we fondly remember. Other memories can be painful or bittersweet. Ultimately, however, most reflection is life-affirming because it results in personal growth and self-discovery. This autobiography describes many types of memories. Some are emotionally charged; others are simple facts of my past. But together they create a pageant I would like to share with you.

While there are many aspects of my life that are telling and rich with meaning for me, I think the most profound experience was earning my graduate diploma in music education at the University of Georgia in Athens, Georgia, in the early years of one of the most tumultuous decades in our nation's history.

As I stood among the other graduate students at the University of Georgia in 1962, the lone African American, to have my degree conferred, I was overcome with emotion. The scene felt surreal. This was truly a watershed moment, both for higher education and for me. After over 175 years of graduating people from the all-white University of Georgia, the institution was about to confer a degree upon an African American.

I surmised that things would never be the same again at UGA. Other Black students—Charlayne Hunter and Hamilton Holmes being the first after me—would follow, and more Blacks would receive degrees in the coming decades.

But as I waited in line I pondered: "How did I get here, to this moment?" I realized that nothing important happens in a vacuum. There had to have been a trigger, a catalyst that set me on this extraordinary path. The trigger in my life, I realized, was a riot. The reader might ask: "How can a riot result in a positive impact on one's life?" Well, I can say it changed my life's trajectory forever. And that change was indeed a positive one, as I became the first African American to receive a diploma from the University of Georgia.

The journey was long—and it begins here.

CHAPTER ONE

Growing Up in Segregated Atlanta: Family Life in the Jim Crow South

I n 1936, Flag Day occurred on a Sunday. I was born on that day. A popular nursery rhyme asserts that "Sunday's child is full of grace." My entrance into the world was accompanied by indignant screams and loud crying. My entry did not indicate much grace.

My parents, Annie Ruth and John Henry Early, were happy to have a healthy, six-pound baby girl. My brother, John, eighteen months older, was not as delighted. When I was brought home, John protested my coming with an abundance of tears. He obviously did not want to share our parents with me. I am told that it took some time before he accepted me as his baby sister. Fortunately, this initial fear was set aside and our family grew to be a close and loving one.

My father was born in Jackson, Georgia, and spent his childhood there. He joined the army at the age of eighteen and served during World War I. After his discharge from the army, he moved to Atlanta. He met and married his first wife. They had one child—Miriam. Dad had a job as a paper cutter at the Southern Wax Paper Company. He was able to purchase a home in Summerhill, a middle-class Black community. Dad and his first wife divorced after twelve years and Miriam and her mother moved away. While visiting in Monroe, Georgia, with a friend, Dad met my mother at a family reunion. After a brief courtship, they moved to Atlanta and married. Mother had worked for several years as a teacher in a one-room schoolhouse. One-room schoolhouses were ubiquitous in rural communities. She loved teaching and had been recommended by her teacher because she was the top student in her class. Mom's teacher was married and was pregnant. Though Mom had not attended college, she was deemed competent enough to teach younger students.

She had embraced her teaching position with relish, but she had always wanted to move to a big city like Atlanta. Now she had her chance. Her new husband had a steady job and a comfortable home, and she looked forward to living in Atlanta and raising her own family.

My earliest recollection about our family's life is that my father owned a restaurant on Auburn Avenue, in an area that was known as the Fourth Ward.

In July 1937, my father must have requested a letter of recommendation from his supervisor at the Southern Wax Paper Company. I found this letter in his papers. It reads: "TO WHOM IT MAY CONCERN: *This is to certify that John H. Early has been in the employ of this company for over eleven years, and he has always been a very efficient and industrious worker. He is a man of splendid character, honest, and of the highest integrity."* The letter was written on company letterhead and signed by J. V. Williamson.

Knowing my father, I assume that he was tired of the poor treatment he received or the menial tasks that Black workers were asked to do. I would guess that he preferred to be self-employed. He probably didn't share that vision with his supervisor, but merely asked for a recommendation.

Dad's restaurant was located at 328 Auburn Avenue, which is part of the Odd Fellows building. He named his establishment the Tuxedo Coffee Shop. I still have a copy of his official business card. As mentioned earlier, the establishment was part of the iconic Fourth Ward. The city of Atlanta was divided into wards at that time. The divisions of the city later changed to districts, but the Fourth Ward retains its original designation. That area of Atlanta is known today as the Old Fourth Ward.

Auburn Avenue represented the epicenter of Black-owned business. It also included major churches, the first Black-owned newspaper (the *Atlanta Daily World*), insurance companies and banks, the only public library for Blacks, nightclubs—and to the north, some family homes. The childhood home of Dr. Martin Luther King Jr. is located on Auburn Ave., as is the MLK National Historic Site. Though Auburn Avenue remains the heart of the Old Fourth Ward, its expanse includes Edgewood, which runs parallel, and its opposite—Ponce de Leon Avenue. This area includes the new Ponce City Market, formerly the old Sears building, and a portion of Atlanta's popular BeltLine.

My brother and I were born during the Great Depression, and we learned much later that African Americans suffered more than whites during those years. Blacks were the first to be laid off from jobs and our unemployment rate was more than twice that of white citizens. President Franklin Delano Roosevelt, a Democrat, tried to alleviate the plight of Black workers through his New Deal project but his policies were often thwarted by southern Democrats. My parents, like most other Blacks, admired Roosevelt for his efforts. Framed photos of Roosevelt (and Abraham Lincoln) graced the walls of our home. I can only assume that my father felt he could succeed better as his own boss during this era.

My mother, though a former teacher, served as one of the restaurant cooks. She was a willowy but strong woman. She was able to transition to the role as cook because she was multitalented. A meticulous housekeeper, she could also cook and greet customers with a smile. She supported our father in the business and raised John and me with love and care at the same time.

My brother and I attended E. P. Johnson Elementary School, which was very close to our home in Summerhill. Though Summerhill was predominantly occupied by Blacks, a sizable enclave of Jewish people also lived there. They owned grocery stores and other businesses in the community. E. P. Johnson, like other Black schools, was so overcrowded that we were always on double sessions; this meant that we went to school for a half day. John and I attended the morning session so that we could go with our mother to the restaurant in the afternoons.

I was a year younger than most of my classmates because I started first grade at the age of five. Perceiving my thirst for learning at an early age, my mother enrolled me in the Gate City private kindergarten when I was four, and I could already read. This was the result of a combination of Mother's teaching us at home and the excellent experiences that I had at the Gate City kindergarten. Mrs. Rachel Brown, principal of E. P. Johnson Elementary school, approved my placement in first grade rather than kindergarten.

LIFE IN SUMMERHILL

Our Summerhill home was a white frame residence—not palatial but well maintained. It had three bedrooms, a large room with French doors that led into the dining room, a kitchen, and one master bathroom upstairs. Later, my dad installed a shower in the basement because one bathroom was simply not sufficient to accommodate the entire family.

My favorite part of the house was the screened-in front porch with a large swing. I loved to curl up in the swing with my favorite books and read. The back porch had steps that led down to the full basement. That was my least favorite area. It was floored with concrete and was cold to bare feet. I didn't like the basement coal cellar because it was dark and scary. Dad had a full-size pool table there and he loved to play pool with my brother. A long, paved driveway ran along the side of the house and ended in a free-standing garage.

We, of course, had no central heating or air conditioning. A coal-burning stove stood in the living room. Mother initially cooked on a wood-burning range in the kitchen. My father later purchased a gas stove for her. The bathroom had a kerosene heater to combat the chill. It, too, was later replaced with a gas heater. The bedrooms were furnished with fireplaces. The windows provided our only air circulation. When the weather became too hot we used cardboard hand-held fans from the local funeral home.

I grew up during World War II. At the height of the war we used blackout curtains at night in the event of enemy bombers. We also had to purchase some food items with ration coupons. Since we had the restaurant, Dad received coupons for home and the business. Meats, sugar, and butter were limited items. Occasionally, Dad took John and me with him to purchase meat for the restaurant and for home. We went to White Provisions for these purchases. It was fascinating to see large portions of meat hanging from huge ceiling hooks. Dad always purchased meat and had it cut to his specifications. After the purchase, he would separate some for use at home. He always made certain that we had a plentiful supply for home use. He had a commercial-style refrigerated meat counter in our basement, which was usually well stocked.

Like most Americans during the war, we had to use a butter substitute. It was a white, waxy substance that had to be colored with an orange dye. It was my job to color the butter substitute, but I refused to eat it. (To this day, I prefer real butter.)

When the war ended in September 1945, everyone was elated. We celebrated at school with the singing of patriotic songs and the waving of small American flags. That day I received my only spanking by Mother because instead of going home from school, I went to a classmate's home for ice cream. Giddy with excitement, I forgot that I needed to get permission from Mother before accepting an invitation. We were late in arriving at the restaurant because of me.

When we went to the restaurant after school, my brother remained there to assist. He was good at math and quickly learned to operate the cash register. I was escorted to the Auburn Avenue Branch Library that was directly across the street from the restaurant. There, I did my homework and read books. I was paid an allowance to "stay out of the way." What a pleasant mode of earning money! And it didn't include washing dishes or polishing furniture. (I did, however, perform those chores at home and kept my bedroom tidy.)

Each month, my brother and I were taken to the downtown First National Bank (now Wells Fargo) to deposit a portion of our allowances. My dad had opened savings accounts for us when we were infants, which meant that at an early age I had been taught the importance of saving money. This was a valuable lesson. My savings later proved handy when I went to Turner High School and needed to purchase a clarinet.

I was an avid reader and a good student. I completed my homework at the library in short order so that I could explore the rich treasure house of books. I think that over time, I read most of the books in the library.

Mrs. Annie L. McPheeters, the librarian, played a pivotal role in my early life. Because I visited the library daily, she took me under her wing. She recommended books from all genres: nonfiction, fiction, travel, biographies, and Negro history. Noting my deep interest in reading, she encouraged me to live vicariously through books. Later, as an adult, I felt honored to receive the McPheeters Professions award from the Auburn

Avenue Research Library. The Auburn Avenue Branch Library, where I spent so much time during my childhood, closed in 1959, leaving me with the feeling that I had lost a friend. But the Auburn Avenue Research Library on African American Culture and History replaced the original Auburn Branch in 1994 and the core collection of the Auburn Branch is housed in this new facility.

During my childhood, the Auburn Avenue Branch (opened in 1921) was the only library that was available for African Americans. We couldn't use the downtown Carnegie Library because, though opened to the public in 1902, it was designated for "whites only." Access to books and printed resources was segregated as were all public facilities in our city. This designation permeated and subverted our experiences in civic life on many levels. Among the memorabilia that I have in my possession is one of my father's business licenses. It is imprinted, in bold blue print, with the words: *For Colored People Only.*

Because I read widely, I excelled. At age eight, my teacher and principal wanted to skip me to the fifth grade. My parents wouldn't allow that move. They said that I was already younger than most of my classmates and they felt that I would suffer socially.

My dad was an unusually astute man. He had only attended elementary school in his birthplace of Jackson, Georgia, but he was very intelligent. I admired his "mother wit." He was forced to quit school to help on his family's sharecropping farm. He always regretted his lack of formal education, but he moved easily among some of Atlanta's Black leaders. His business acumen and his passion for golfing probably earned him this acceptance. Though respected as an equal, he was always sensitive to his lack of education. He insisted that my brother and I work hard in school. He and our mother felt that education was key to the progress of Black people and they had lofty aspirations for us. I often wondered, when I was older, what our parents might have accomplished had they been able to attend college.

My mom, though hired as teacher in a one-room schoolhouse in Monroe in Walton County, Georgia, had only finished high school. Mother was a capable teacher. She once told me, however, that she was often frustrated because her older students could not attend school daily.

During harvesting season, the older students had to drop out of school to work on their parents' or white landowners' farms. This resulted in frequent customization of content for the older students. It made her job much more difficult. Teaching all grades in one room must have been a daunting task.

At home, she was really our first teacher. We always had books, magazines, and newspapers in our home. I enjoyed curling up on the bed and hearing her read to us at night. She read to us initially but we were expected to read ourselves when we were old enough to do so.

MY FATHER'S ENTHUSIASMS AND LESSONS FOR US CHILDREN

My father was a golf enthusiast and after he closed the family's restaurant in 1947, he served as manager of the Lincoln Golf and Country Club—one of the first and most influential golf clubs for Black people in the Southeast. He went to the golf club each morning and returned home at 5:00 p.m. for dinner. In her new role at home Mom enjoyed doing housework, cooking, sewing, or reading books and newspapers.

Dad had asked to purchase the building where our restaurant was located, but the owner didn't want to sell it, so the restaurant business ended in 1947. It had served our family well; however, John and I were happy when it closed because we could stay at home and enjoy a more "normal" childhood with time for us all to be together. Also, with the restaurant closed, this meant we could play outside with our friends after school and on weekends. We enjoyed playing outdoors in the sun and fresh air. What a joy! The girls played ring games or circle games. Some games included singing; other games included chants and clapping partners' hands or making dramatic movements. Our favorites included "Miss Mary Mack," "Charlie over the Water," and "Aunt Jenny Died." Playing hopscotch and jumping rope provided the exercise that we needed, while the rhyme games honed our hand-and-eye coordination and musical skills.

The boys mostly played marbles or football and volleyball. They rarely played with the girls. We children were allowed to play outside as long as we remained on the sidewalks or in the yards.

I could tell what Mom was cooking—even when I was playing outside. The wonderful fragrances that emanated from the kitchen whetted my appetite. I basked in the fresh, woodsy smell of green beans bubbling on the stove. I could also identify collard greens by their pungent odor. Though we ate a variety of vegetables, these two were my favorites. We also were treated to a variety of meats: succulent beef roast, golden-brown fried chicken, or steak were Sunday entrees. Weekdays she offered pork chops, spaghetti and meat sauce, fried liver (not my favorite), neck bones or various casserole dishes.

My father loved rabbit meat and would sometimes ask Mom to cook rabbit for dinner, which occasionally raised some concern on my part. John and I owned two pet rabbits. My rabbit was named Bugs Ella, and John's was Bugs Bunny. We enjoyed playing with our rabbits, though we disliked cleaning the hutch.

I remember once crying over my dinner and refusing to eat rabbit, which served as the entree. I told my dad that it was Bugs Ella's cousin, and that I just couldn't eat it. Dad smiled and told me to eat my vegetables. He even allowed me to eat some peach pie for dessert.

We didn't eat desserts every day, but Mom cooked delicious fruit pies or banana pudding occasionally. We also enjoyed homemade ice cream and cake on special occasions.

When I was tired of playing outside I loved to sit in the kitchen and watch my mother cooking, awed by her culinary skills. At her side I learned to cook various dishes but enjoyed most the creation of pies and cakes. Mom knew that I didn't like to eat liver—so she taught me to cook a chicken liver casserole. It was a simple recipe that included chicken livers, rice, and a cream chicken soup in layers. I enjoyed cooking this casserole because it was very tasty. Her patient lessons still inspire me today.

We had a large backyard with flowering pear and peach trees. This space was shared with some pet ducks, including one who loved to frighten me and chase me back to the house. Dad built a duck pond in our yard and the ducks loved to splash, paddle, and play in it. He had done well in the restaurant business because he was very frugal; during this time, we were able to live comfortably even though he wasn't working at a full-time job.

Not surprisingly, Dad wanted John and me to enjoy the game of golf as he did. He purchased child-sized golf bags for both of us. They were, of course, outfitted with the appropriate clubs. I loved the heady fragrance of the leather golf bag but disliked the game. I saw no sense in knocking a ball away from you only to knock it away again. My brother, however, took to the game immediately. He served as Dad's caddy and continued to enjoy golf in his adult years.

The only concession that I made to my father's passion was to serve as announcer during club tournaments. Dad played golf with many friends, including H. M. Holmes. Dr. Holmes was Hamilton Holmes's grandfather and a noted Atlanta physician. He was also an early civil rights activist, leading a campaign to integrate Atlanta's golf courses. Under his leadership, golf courses became the first desegregated public facilities in Atlanta.

Dad also played with "Nish" Williams who was Don Clendenon's stepfather and a noted baseball coach and player. (Don Clendenon, a Morehouse College graduate, later became a famous baseball player. He played with the Pittsburgh Pirates and the New York Mets and was named MVP when the Mets won the World Series in 1969.)

I remember one incident during my childhood when Don was visiting our home. We were in our spacious backyard, and John was demonstrating how to execute a proper golf swing. Don, six months younger than my brother, swung the golf club back so far that he struck my brother in the cheek. When I saw John's bloody cheek, I jumped onto Don's back and began to pummel him. Mom came out when she heard John's screams of pain and stopped my assault. Of course, we had a trip to the hospital to get stitches in John's cheek.

It's fortunate that Don Clendenon went on to become an outstanding baseball player rather than a golfer. And it's even more fortunate that I later embraced the philosophy of nonviolence.

Though I never took up the game of golf as a personal sport, I did learn much from my dad about the game. Not only did I learn the terminology, such as "birdie," "albatross," "bogey," "handicap," and so on, I also learned that one should play for the joy of the game. He told me that one plays in competition with oneself and that this is what one should do in any career.

My father's volunteer manager position at the Lincoln Golf and Country Club lasted for two years before he embarked on another business venture.

While family life was absolutely the core of our life experience, institutional education was the most influential force guiding my brother and me into the larger world. We embarked on this journey with unceasing support from our parents and while we never "left" our family, we would venture into the broader world as students of public education, curious about our world and society at large.

LIVING UNDER THE THUMB OF JIM CROW IN THE AMERICAN SOUTH

Though our parents tried to shelter John and me from the ignominies of segregation, we couldn't escape them entirely. Segregation and the indignities caused by Jim Crow laws were a constant reminder that our country still needed to evolve and mature into a true democracy. Our family chose to reject these odious rules by dedicating ourselves to hard work, improving ourselves through education, and nurturing our love for one another. Sadly, the frustrations of Jim Crow were ubiquitous.

Jim Crow laws forced us to sit at the back of the streetcar when traveling to the restaurant or to downtown stores. We sat at the back of the bus when traveling to our grandmother's home in Monroe. We couldn't go to downtown movies, though a few movie houses accepted Blacks in segregated sections. We were restricted to the two movie houses for colored citizens. The Ashby Theater was in northwest Atlanta; the Royal Theater was in northeast Atlanta. Fortunately, the Royal Theater was located on Auburn Avenue, not far from our restaurant. John and I were permitted to attend movies there occasionally. I enjoyed the cartoons, but John preferred the western movies. I admit that I, too, enjoyed *The Lone Ranger* and *Roy Rogers* movies.

When John and I were older, Mother allowed us to go to the downtown Fox Theater. Colored patrons were not allowed to use the front entrance. We had to go to the Ponce de Leon side entrance. The ticket kiosk was on the street level. After purchasing a ticket, we had to climb several flights of outdoor stairs to get to our seats. Colored patrons sat in an upper balcony that was above the white balcony. A thick wall separated the two areas. I was so upset over the demeaning entrance and seating arrangement that I didn't enjoy the movie. I felt, and John shared my feeling, that no movie was worth the shame of such treatment. When we returned home, Mom asked if we had enjoyed the movie. We told her that we had not and our reason. She was already aware of what we would encounter but wanted us to experience the degrading situation for ourselves. We learned a valuable lesson and never returned to the Fox Theater during our childhood. The experience haunted me in ways I could not have expected: The balloon-like ceiling was so close to our heads that I had recurring nightmares about the ceiling falling and smothering us.

Later, in the mid-seventies, the Fox Theater suffered a decline and was destined to be demolished. A massive fundraising campaign was initiated to "Save the Fox." Most Black citizens, including me, declined to contribute to this campaign for the historic building. The painful memory of my childhood experience still resonated in my mind. I didn't care if the Fox was demolished. The fundraising was successful and the Fox was saved, but not with my help. The first time that I entered the Fox again was in my late adult life when I attended an Alvin Ailey dance concert. The Alvin Ailey company, a prestigious modern dance troupe, represents the best of the American dream. This outstanding dance company, though originally all African American, boasts talented dancers of all ethnicities. I wanted to attend this concert because it negates all that the Fox Theater once represented.

I also remember when the New York Metropolitan Opera came to Atlanta. The Fox Theater presented elaborate opera productions to Atlanta's white elite audiences. Initially, Blacks were only allowed to serve as ushers or restroom maids. Dr. Killingsworth, our department chair at Clark College, which I would later attend, encouraged the music majors to volunteer as ushers. I never took his advice because I didn't want to attend unless I could go as an audience member. Finally, Rudolf Bing, the Met's director, rebelled against Atlanta's segregation laws and moved his opera troupe to the Civic Center. That venue did not appeal to the white audience and so the Met discontinued its annual tour to Atlanta. Bing was also upset because his occasional Black singers could not go to the Georgian Terrace Hotel where the white singers were feted with lavish meals. Black singers could not participate in the elaborate events held at private, white-only driving clubs (country clubs). These establishments simply refused to relax their segregation laws that barred Blacks and Jews.

Other restrictions accorded to Black citizens were equally demeaning. Except for the few Black-owned establishments located in Black communities, we couldn't eat in the city's restaurants. Neither could we try on clothing in the stores; we had simply to look at items to determine if they were the correct size. If something didn't fit when we tried clothing on at home, we could not return it. Though Mother was an excellent seamstress, she did not have the time to sew clothes for us with her job at the restaurant. She did, occasionally, make a few dresses for me. When purchasing shoes, we always had to sit at the back of the store.

Public restroom facilities were rarely available and water fountains were labeled "colored" and "white." As a child, I often wondered if the "white" water tasted different from the "colored" water. At that time, however, I never had the courage to drink from the water fountains for whites. I wondered, too, why we couldn't use public water since our parents paid city taxes. It was not only confusing, but also upsetting to our young minds.

Housing was also segregated. My family lived on Terry Street in southeast Atlanta. The Summerhill community was near where the Turner baseball stadium (now a Georgia State University stadium) stands today.

ASPIRING TO EXPERIENCE AMERICA
DURING THE JIM CROW ERA

Experiencing the world beyond our family life and local neighborhoods and institutions is one of the most important aspects of being a full citizen. But traveling long distances by car in America was quite difficult for Black people in the early to mid-twentieth century. Unlike today, Black citizens could not just make reservations at any hotel. They could not stop at the first convenient restaurant when hunger overtook them. Restroom facilities were often not available at service stations. "Sundown" towns warned Black travelers that they would invite trouble if found in those towns after dark.

African American travelers, however, always exhibited resilience and ingenuity when on the road. Most families would take their own food rather than spend time en route looking for a friendly restaurant. Fancy picnic baskets were generally not used; shoe boxes and other portable containers were used instead. Popular dishes included fried chicken, deviled eggs, cake, cookies, and soft drinks. Foods that were easily spoiled by the heat or time in the car were avoided. Travel itineraries were carefully planned to include stopovers at the homes of family or friends rather than hotels. The problems of food and hotels were solved with the forward vision of one very wise African American.

In 1936, Victor Hugo Green, a well-educated Black man from New York City, published his first volume of *The Negro Motorist Green Book*, covering the New York area. This very useful book listed hotels, private or "tourist" homes, restaurants, and service stations that would welcome Black travelers. After the initial year, Green expanded the coverage to include other states. The book was published annually through 1966 except for the war years. It was needed because motoring was less expensive than flying or riding the train or bus, and those options presented their own Jim Crow problems for Black travelers. (Victor Hugo Green died in 1960; his wife continued to update and publish the book until 1966.)

Though my parents worked long hours at the restaurant, we managed to get away occasionally for some rest and relaxation. While my father never purchased a Green Book, to my knowledge, he did experience problems in traveling by automobile. And my mother and I had difficulties in riding the Greyhound bus to Monroe, Georgia, approximately 60 miles from Atlanta. I will never forget one memorable trip we took together.

MOTHER AND I VENTURE OUTSIDE OF ATLANTA

One day, Mother said that she would take me to Monroe to visit with my maternal grandmother for whom I was named. Grandmother Mary was the only grandparent that I knew. My maternal grandfather died before I was born. I never knew my father's parents because they, too, had died before my birth. Many of my cousins still live in Monroe. (My grandmother Mary had six children.) Over the years, some married and moved away. We didn't have big family reunions during my formative years, as people do today, so visits are strong memories for me. For the most part, my Monroe cousins were farming the land during my early life while my immediate family was busy in Atlanta with the restaurant and then the grocery store. There was no time to get away for large family reunions, which became more common in the latter part of the twentieth century. I am thankful for the extended family I still have in Monroe and enjoy seeing the next generations taking on new challenges.

For this particular trip to Monroe, my brother John stayed to help Father at the restaurant and because my mother didn't drive, we went downtown to the Greyhound bus station for the trip. I was eight years of age and thrilled about the bus trip. Traveling by bus was a rare experience for me because we usually traveled in my father's automobile. I was excited about a new adventure out in the world with my mother.

When she and I boarded the bus, my mother gave the bus driver our tickets and steered me to the middle section of the vehicle. The prevailing Jim Crow law demanded that Blacks had to sit at the back, but there weren't many passengers on the bus and plenty of empty seats were available. When the burly bus driver noticed us sitting together, he lumbered down the aisle and said to me: "You can't sit beside this white woman." My mother had a very fair complexion with naturally straight hair. (I always admired my mother's long, straight hair. She only had to wash and dry it—and it remained straight. As a child, my hair was worn natural, in plaits. Later, during my teen years, I was allowed to have it straightened with a hot comb.) I was also darker than my mother. I looked at him and said: "But she's my mother!" My mother said nothing. She just put her arms around me and we hugged. The bus driver's face turned beet red, and he walked back up the aisle.

When we arrived in Monroe, my uncle Orell picked us up and drove us to Grandmother's home. I tearfully told my uncle what had happened on the bus. He patted me on the shoulder and told me that it was okay for me to cry. I ran to hug my grandmother when we arrived at her home. Grandmother Mary asked me why I had been crying. Mother explained what had happened. She told her mother that this was what she dreaded when we had to travel by bus. She also said that she and my dad tried to avoid these upsetting incidents with the children. Grandmother Mary told her that she couldn't shelter us from all unpleasantness because we lived in the South.

I learned much later in life that my grandmother was sired by the white foreman who owned the farm where my great-grandmother worked as a slave. Grandmother Mary was very fair like my mother. She also had naturally straight hair. I now have a grainy photo of Grandmother Mary. She is pictured with her two "white" sisters. They all look very much alike. I now realize that my grandmother had experienced the degradation of segregation and miscegenation firsthand. As a child I didn't understand the complex situation with white men and Black female workers, and I have never forgotten that humiliating bus experience.

A FAMILY TRIP TO FLORIDA

A similar incident occurred when my father took the family with him to Florida. He was participating in a golf tournament and wanted us to accompany him.

Since we didn't experience many vacations because of responsibilities at the restaurant, John and I were ecstatic about the prospect of a trip to Florida. The drive, in my father's new Buick, was very pleasant. John and I enjoyed seeing the bucolic scenes of pecan groves, cotton fields, and small towns as we rolled down the highway. As city kids, we didn't often experience the opportunity to view these scenes.

After a while, we stopped at a small-town service station to refuel. Mother and I needed to use the restroom. Dad asked the attendant where the ladies' restroom was located. The white attendant told him that they didn't have facilities for "[n-word]." My father directed him to siphon out the gas that had been pumped. He told the man that he didn't do business with places that practiced this type of discrimination.

My mother and I were frightened because we knew that my dad had a shotgun in the trunk of the car. We also knew that he would not hesitate to use it if necessary. Mother begged Dad to get back into the car. He finally did, and we drove away. Sadly, my mother and I had to use the roadside bushes for a restroom. We stopped at another service station and refilled the gas tank, then rode on to Florida.

I don't remember much about the golf tournament, but the incident at the first service station was imprinted on my young mind. Such was life in the Jim Crow South where we lived. In the introduction to his first guidebook, Victor Hugo Green wrote: "There will be a day, sometime in the near future, when this guide will not have to be published. That is when we as a race will have equal rights and privileges in the United States."

Thank God that we do have equal rights today, though they are not always acknowledged. Travel for Blacks today is not much of a problem thanks to the laws that were finally enacted. (We are also indebted to the 1960s Freedom Riders who risked life and limb to ensure that the laws were enforced. These were the civil rights activists who took interstate buses all over the South to challenge the nonenforcement of the Supreme Court rulings that made segregated bus rides unconstitutional.) Victor Hugo Green's vision has finally been realized. He, unfortunately, did not live to experience it.

A footnote to this narrative is the fact that Dad traveled by plane to Chicago in the late 1930s. I have a yellowed copy of a newspaper article entitled "Atlantan Who Travelled to Golf Meet in Plane Back." The article does not include a byline for the reporter's name. The article was published in the *Atlanta Daily World* on September 12, 1938. I also found a brochure describing a United Golfers Association meet held in Chicago in August/September 1938. The article states that my father flew to Chicago on an American Airways plane for a golf meet. The plane left Atlanta from Candler Field. This was Atlanta's only airfield at that time. The reporter asserts that Dad was hosted by a Chicago friend and enjoyed several events held in his honor. These celebratory events were in addition to his participating in the golf meet. He spent a week in Chicago and returned home on the Dixie Flyer train. I can't imagine that my father was able to afford a plane trip to Chicago in 1938 and I will always wonder how he was treated on the plane and the train. It is telling that today this would not be at the forefront of our concerns for loved ones taking a trip.

ADVENTURING NORTH TO NEW YORK CITY

My own personal experiences in traveling in planes and trains, however, provide a clue. I celebrated my seventeenth birthday two weeks after I'd graduated from Turner High School. My mother surprised me with a train ticket to New York City as a graduation gift. She told me that I was invited to visit my half-sister, Miriam, who lived in Brooklyn. She was seventeen years older than me, and I didn't know her well. She had married and moved to New York after I was born.

I was excited about going to the big city of New York! I'd never traveled by train before, and this was a new adventure for me. I was proud that my mother trusted me enough to allow me to travel alone on the train. Miriam was to meet me at Penn Station in New York and take me to her home in Brooklyn.

Since my visit was to extend to two weeks, I carefully prepared what I would take for clothes. I had received a new set of sky blue luggage as a graduation gift. I packed every nook and cranny of my luggage except for my train case. My mom had decided that I would take food items in the case for my journey. We knew that the dining car did not accept Black travelers.

On the day of my departure, my mom took me to the Terminal Station for the trip. I was to ride on the Silver Comet train, which was popular at that time. I tearfully bid my mother good-bye and boarded the train. I noticed that there were two partitioned compartments: one for white passengers, and one for Blacks. The Black compartment was in front, just behind the engine. The white compartment was behind the Black section. It led to the dining car, the observation car, and the sleeper section. Our compartment did not have luggage racks, so luggage had to be stored beneath the seat and in the aisle. I held my train case in my lap so that I could partake of its delicacies when I was hungry.

The train rolled through the countryside and through large cities. The trip to New York took twelve hours, but I enjoyed looking out the window and seeing more of America than I'd seen before.

Though I'd had a hearty breakfast (at my mother's insistence), I became hungry. I opened my case and marveled at the wonderful meal that she had prepared for me. It included fried chicken, potato salad and deviled eggs packed in ice, some fruit, two slices of cake, a small box of cookies, and a Coca-Cola. I was in heaven! I noticed that other passengers were also eating their "take-along" meals. At that moment, I didn't care that Blacks were not allowed to use the dining car. My mother's cooking could rival that of any other cook.

After eating my lunch, I fell asleep—but with some difficulty. The stiff, upright seats were not conducive to comfortable sleeping. Mother had insisted that I pack a bulky sweater because the weather might turn cold. She also said that I could use it for a pillow. I silently thanked my mom for her wisdom, pulled out my sweater, and fell asleep. The train also boasted a sleeper car, but again, Blacks were not allowed this luxury. It puzzled me to know that Blacks could serve as Pullman porters, red caps, waiters, and cooks, but could not take advantage of the amenities that trains afforded.

When I woke, the twelve-hour journey was still not over. Dusk was falling, and the blurry scenes flew by without much definition. Bored, I pulled out one of my books and began to read. Shortly after 7:00 p.m., the train slowed and pulled into Penn Station.

I was instantly overwhelmed by the huge crowds and the massive station. My sister had sent a photo of herself so that I could recognize her. As I stepped off the train, she rushed to me, hugged me tightly, and told me to follow her. We waded through the crowds and finally arrived at the garage where her car was parked. I had thought that Atlanta was a big city, but it couldn't compare with New York. Taxi cabs honked their horns, hordes of people rushed up and down the streets, neon signs blinked a panoply of brilliant colors—it was just too much to absorb. The trip to Brooklyn took a while to maneuver.

When we reached Miriam's brownstone apartment, I was amazed at how close the apartments were to each other. They all looked the same, and packed side to side as they were, I wondered how anyone knew which was theirs.

Miriam's apartment was upstairs, but thankfully, there was an elevator. I was pleased to see the tastefully decorated interior of Miriam's home. She had divorced her husband and lived alone. Miriam had prepared a dinner for me, but I was too weary to eat. She showed me to her second bedroom. I pulled my pajamas from my suitcase, changed, collapsed on the bed, and fell asleep.

Miriam was an excellent hostess. She had planned several interesting adventures for me. We attended a Broadway play, viewed breathtaking sights from atop the Empire State Building, went to Coney Island, boarded a yacht to do deep-sea fishing, attended two movies, and sailed to Liberty Island to admire the iconic Statue of Liberty. During these exhilarating ventures we got to know each other better.

I marveled at the huge library that was not segregated. I also loved Central Park and the Central Park Zoo. The art museums provided new avenues of cultural awareness that I had never experienced. Miriam cooked most of our meals, but I was astonished that we could eat at restaurants that did not discriminate on the basis of race. I found New York a fascinating city and vowed to return some day to see more of this new world. I suspect this first trip to New York on my own planted the seed of the love of travel that I would enjoy later in life.

My return trip home was quite uneventful because I had seen so much and had so much to tell my family and friends. The racial limitations of traveling on the train, however, continued to disturb me. I found it difficult to understand why the South was so discriminatory. I did understand, however, that the Mason-Dixon line, the boundary that separated the slave and free states, remained a reality.

MY FIRST AIRPLANE TRIP

My first plane trip occurred five years later in 1958. I flew to Traverse City, Michigan, to attend the National Music Camp at Interlochen. This camp included a division of the University of Michigan where I wanted to pursue a master's degree.

I have a photo of me coming down the steps of the plane. (There were no jetways at that time.) I was wearing a suit, a small hat, and high heels. In those days, passengers' attire was more professional when they flew. It was nothing like today when some passengers wear flip-flops, shorts, and T-shirts. Treatment of Blacks, however, was similar to the train ride that I experienced in 1953. Black passengers were seated at the back of the plane. First-class seating was not allowed even if one could afford it.

While the Civil Rights Act was passed in 1964, it took several years before it was strictly enforced—particularly in the South. The freedom to travel like any other U.S. citizen was a freedom Black people could not take for granted, and we have to wonder how these humiliations and frustrations shaped our society or held it back.

Although these situations were very common and ubiquitous in everyday life, our parents never taught us to hate, dislike, or disrespect white people. We were taught instead to love everyone and to respect all people—especially the elderly. On a fundamental, human level we detested the Jim Crow laws. Unfortunately, segregation was pervasive and endemic throughout Atlanta and the entire South.

My brother and I, however, were taught that we were equal to anyone and could accomplish anything that we were prepared to do. Education represented the pathway to our personal success. We were also taught to believe in ourselves and in our abilities, and to set goals for ourselves. These lessons were usually taught when we sat together for meals. Our parents promised a better future for John and me and that promise was instilled in us in numerous ways, but it started with self-respect and then reached outward to an understanding of living a life beyond the confines of the unethical and soul-destroying "laws" of Jim Crow.

CHAPTER TWO

My Education: Beginnings

EARLY MUSIC EDUCATION AND
E. P. JOHNSON ELEMENTARY SCHOOL

When I was attending E. P. Johnson Elementary School, I had no idea of the genesis of its naming. I discovered much later that it was because of the legacy of Edwin Posey Johnson. He served as the pastor of the iconic Reed Street Baptist Church, which was located close to my home. Later in life I learned that Rev. Dr. Johnson received his education in the first graduating class of Atlanta University. He earned the doctor of divinity degree at the Atlanta Baptist Seminary and taught theology at Morehouse College. He was active in Atlanta, state, and national Christian organizations. Under Dr. Johnson's leadership, the imposing stone Reed Street Baptist Church was completed in 1910. The Summerhill elementary school was named in his honor because of his work in the church, community, and across the state. I feel privileged to have attended this outstanding school that was named in his honor. My elementary school years proved to be a pivotal part of my lifelong participation in music and music education, though of course I wasn't thinking of this at the time.

The days under the supervision of Mrs. Jessie Wartman, music supervisor at E. P. Johnson Elementary School, were fundamental to my life's journey. Mrs. Wartman worked at our school and other Black schools in the city system. She came to our school periodically during the school year and taught us singing, how to read music notation, and some basic music theory. Though her singing voice was rather high-pitched and could make our small ears ache, I enjoyed those periodic lessons and looked forward to each of her school visits. I remember that when I was in the third grade, we used a small green music textbook: *The Music Hour*. Mrs. Wartman told us that the book was dedicated to Lowell Mason and that he was called the father of public school music. She also said that he was the first music teacher in Boston, Massachusetts, and was responsible for music education being taught in all of Boston's public schools. I don't know how I acquired a book, but I still have a copy of this seminal music text. It was published in 1829 by Silver Burdett.

Under her direction our school participated in an all-city Black music festival that was held at the Atlanta Municipal Auditorium, or City Auditorium as we called it. This was exciting for us children as this auditorium was where so much of the city's entertainment took place for many decades, from concerts to conventions. We felt as if we were part of something much bigger when we performed there. I was in the third grade at the time and among those who performed in the rhythm band. The festival included hundreds of students representing each of the Black elementary schools with a chorus, a rhythm band, an elementary band with traditional instruments, and a dance troupe. It was truly a gala event.

While I enjoyed playing in the rhythm band, where we wore a special white uniform that included a little round hat, I really wanted to play in the elementary band with traditional instruments. I thought that its harmonized selections sounded more pleasant than the rhythms that we performed. Perhaps I recognized in the band's performance more of what I wanted to strive for?

In any case, after the festival I asked Mrs. Wartman why I couldn't play in a real band. She told me that I was chosen for the rhythm band because I could read the rhythms and that I should be proud of my ability. She also explained that our schools did not all have band instruction because of the expense. E. P. Johnson's limited budget was not adequate to fund band instruments and a male itinerant band teacher. Mrs. Wartman's preparation and skills were strictly vocal. She could not teach band.

I was crestfallen but determined that I would join a real band when I went to high school. I never forgot this promise to myself and followed through with my dream. In some ways I think that this sense of determination followed me throughout my life, giving me an inner strength that made it possible for me to face some of the societal barriers of my race with grace. It helped knowing what I liked, what I wanted, and where my talents lay.

What were my earliest influences? How did I get to where I am today—a retired music educator with a lifelong love of the power of music? My father, an amateur singer, often sang at church and at social events. His favorite song was "Trees" (lyrics by Joyce Kilmer). I still have a tattered copy of the sheet music that he autographed for me, which serves as a totem of his significance in my choice of careers. Also, I began taking piano lessons at the age of nine. We had a stately upright piano at home. It sat prominently in the living room and I enjoyed playing it.

Aware of my interest in music, my parents arranged for piano lessons from Professor B. L. Byron. His piano studio was upstairs in the same building as our restaurant. Always dressed in a suit and tie, Professor Byron radiated the aura of a professional performer. He was thorough in his teaching, and he insisted on complete accuracy in my playing. It was clear to me that if I didn't take my playing seriously, he would not be willing to teach me.

I looked forward to those weekly piano lessons and also liked the musty smell that emanated from the pile of books and sheet music atop Professor Byron's piano. Though enjoying his teaching, I didn't like the fact that he hit me on my knuckles with a pencil when I made a mistake. After two years of study, I told my parents that I had to stop taking lessons. I explained that my knuckles couldn't bear the punishment any longer.

My father wanted me to continue because he expected me to be able to accompany him when he sang. He didn't, however, insist. Instead, he purchased a set of the *International Library of Music*, a 16-volume set of piano books. In addition to classical compositions, it included technical exercises, music history, and music theory. The not-so-subtle hint was that I should continue my piano studies, albeit on my own rather than with a teacher.

Although my formal lessons were over, I continued to practice at home whenever I had some free time. Using the skills that Professor

Byron had taught, I dutifully practiced scales, technical exercises, and as many of the easier classical compositions that I could play. After the two years of formal piano lessons, I was basically self-taught until I resumed lessons in the eleventh grade. Occasionally, I sought the help of a neighbor, Mrs. Mary Williams, who lived across the street from our home. She coached me in learning to play simple hymns, such as "Amazing Grace," which remains one of my favorite hymns today. I used the International Library of Music books throughout my college career and still have most of them today.

Another reason I wanted to discontinue piano lessons was a secret that I kept from my parents: I found it difficult to see the printed music. My vision was very poor. Perhaps that is partly why I made mistakes during lessons.

In fifth grade I couldn't see what our teacher wrote on the blackboard. Instead of telling my parents about this problem, I asked a classmate to write on my notebook what was written on the blackboard. I would give the classmate some candy that I'd snitched from home as a bribe. When the teacher discovered what I was doing, she told my mother that I had a vision problem, which resulted in our going to an ophthalmologist. I was diagnosed with myopia or nearsightedness. To my dismay, I had to wear glasses, but the life span of that first pair was short-lived.

At the end of one long day at the restaurant, we ate fish sandwiches in my parents' room. It was a cold and blustery night, and we ate in front of the blazing fireplace. The sandwiches were wrapped in paper. I took my glasses off and placed them on my lap. When I finished eating the sandwich, I balled the paper (along with my glasses) and threw it into the blazing fire.

I panicked when I couldn't find my glasses and told my parents what had apparently happened. The thoroughly melted glasses were found in the fire, and I received a scolding for my carelessness.

We went to the optometrist to purchase a replacement pair. I confess that while I didn't like the glasses, I really didn't do this on purpose.

My love of classical music began during my childhood days and I wanted to be able to attend live performances. But the Jim Crow laws in Atlanta included all cultural events and I was particularly disappointed that we couldn't attend symphony concerts at the City Auditorium. My father, however, solved that problem. He gathered the entire family together on Sunday evenings to listen to the Bell Telephone Hour on the radio. Those programs, broadcast by NBC, featured classical, light classical, and Broadway music. We enjoyed our concerts at home and learned much about classical music. I fondly remember those family gatherings on Sunday evenings.

Another favorite family tradition happened just before the Christmas holidays. My parents purchased cases of apples, oranges, assorted candies, and paper bags. John and I, under Mother's supervision, filled the bags with fruit and candies. Singing Christmas carols together made the task more fun. Mom didn't possess a great voice, but she joined in and sang lustily. She also taught us new carols when we exhausted our repertoire.

We then distributed the bags to neighbors and other children as Christmas gifts. This fun-filled tradition, inspired with music of the season, supported our learning to share with others. Even today, I enjoy shopping for Christmas and other special day gifts for family and friends.

My love of education outside the home began with going to E. P. Johnson Elementary. Though our school lacked many of the amenities that were included in white schools, our education was first rate. Unfortunately, there was little parity between the white and the "colored" schools. In his 1972 book *From Ivy Street to Kennedy Center: A Centennial History of the Atlanta Public School System*, author Melvin W. Ecke noted that in 1946–1947, the Atlanta Public Schools spent $139.73 for each white student and $59.86 for each African American student. This resulted in our elementary school having no lunchroom facility, no playground equipment, no well-stocked library, and no current textbooks. Our textbooks were always discarded used books from white schools when they received new ones. Our books had names of the white schools stamped in the front, and often had torn or missing pages, which was rather disheartening for those of us eager to learn.

We had, however, dedicated teachers who broadened our horizons with excellent teaching. Black teachers were paid less than their white counterparts, of course, but that fact was not reflected in their teaching.

This was a time when there were no classes for special needs students. All children at each grade level studied in the same classroom environment—whatever their ability.

Corporal punishment was still allowed. I remember that when classmates came to school without their homework, our sixth-grade teacher would call the errant students to the front of the class. They were told to bend over a bench that was placed at center front. They receive several licks from a yardstick. I didn't want to experience that humiliation or the pain—so I always did my homework.

MY INTELLECTUAL AWAKENING BEGINS

We never studied Negro history because it was not part of the prescribed curriculum. But when I was in seventh grade our teacher, Miss Jeanne Willis, decided that we would read a text that was entitled *Ethiopia at the Bar of Justice* (*Plays and Pageants from the Life of the Negro* by Willis Richardson, 1930). This play, or pageant, had a big effect on me.

Later in life, I purchased a facsimile copy of this book because its contents still resonated in my mind. Willis Richardson stated in the book's introduction that the problems in compiling the twelve plays or pageants included in the book were threefold: Each selection must be written by a Negro; must contain no dialect; and must be suitable for audiences of schoolchildren, churches, or theaters. The famed Carter G. Woodson, founder of Negro History Week in America, served as editor for the book.

Richardson noted that *Ethiopia at the Bar of Justice* was written by Edward P. McCoo, an A.M.E. minister. McCoo originally produced the play for an A.M.E. church conference in 1924. The pageant was received with an enthusiastic response and became a favorite vehicle for teaching the strivings and accomplishments of the Negro race. Knowing this helped me to better understand why Miss Willis selected it for our seventh-grade class.

The play portrayed the white race as the character Opposition, and the Black race as the character Ethiopia. The text began with Opposition declaring that Ethiopia had done nothing to advance America's civilization. I was assigned the character of Mercy, defendant for Ethiopia. Many characters including History, Business, Crispus Attucks, Veterans of several wars, Slaves, Professions, the Declaration of Independence, Thirteenth, Fourteenth, Fifteenth Amendments, the church, Womanhood, and several others came forth to sing the praises of Ethiopia. They related the story of the many contributions that Ethiopia had made to America. The pageant ended with Justice embracing Ethiopia and banishing Opposition. Though Music was not one of the playwright's characters, it is interspersed throughout the pageant. The finale featured the singing of "The Star-Spangled Banner" by the entire cast. Our class not only read the pageant, we proudly presented it as a school play for our parents and the community. The pageant stirred us with a sense of empowerment and self-esteem. It was a way to articulate that although we lived in an era of constraining Jim Crow laws, Blacks excelled in helping to make America great.

That pageant signaled my awakening to the many contributions of the Black race. Its central message made a powerful impact on my youthful life. It also presaged my future as a civil rights activist. In a sense, it started me on my journey to UGA, though I didn't know it at that time.

Miss Willis was my favorite teacher while I was in elementary school. She was from Canada and exhibited a more liberal approach to our studies; she was not afraid to enhance and embellish the prescribed curriculum. Perhaps that shaped her plans to marry at the end of the school year and move to another state.

She told us that her grandparents, during the slave-owning era in the United States, fled to Canada via the Underground Railroad. She had returned to get her education because she'd heard glowing reports about Spelman College in Atlanta. We were privileged to have a recent Spelman graduate with a major in English literature. She introduced us to the wonders of Black poetry as well as the conventional poetry of the time. As part of our instruction we had to memorize poems and recite them in class. I was assigned the poem "Daffodils" by William Wordsworth, as well as "The Negro Speaks of Rivers" by Langston Hughes.

I loved to recite both and reveled in the joy of being inspired by Black poets in addition to those of the white race. Hearing the poets' voices through their writing somehow made their humanity (rather than their "race") all the more moving.

In a recent conversation with classmate Rosa Rice Hadley, I was reminded of our competition to be valedictorian at E. P. Johnson Elementary. She had attended for only one year because she transferred there as a seventh-grader and was an avid learner like me. She might have triumphed over me had she attended more than one year. In our conversation we discussed our experiences at E. P. Johnson, specifically the principal who had succeeded Mrs. Brown when she retired. We agreed that Mrs. Sammye E. Coan had an entirely different personality from her predecessor. Mrs. Coan, though an excellent principal, was rather strict and reserved. I told Rosa that, ironically, I had ended up teaching at the middle school that was named after Mrs. Coan. Rosa and I enjoyed our last year of elementary school. I think that she attended Washington High when I went to Howard High. I don't know where she attended college, but it was probably Spelman. Both of us chose teaching as our careers.

Rosa also told me that her mother had assisted my mom in crafting May Day costumes for our class. Since my mother had served as the lone seamstress before that year, I am certain that she was grateful for the help. Both of our mothers were heavily involved at our school. (When I joined the teaching profession, I really appreciated their efforts. Parental involvement always results in a stronger school.)

The pageant's impact continued to resonate in my mind. After promotion to high school, I introduced *Ethiopia at the Bar of Justice* to fellow teens at Mount Vernon Baptist Church where I was a member. We proudly presented it to the whole congregation. I wanted my peers and their parents to be aware of the rich legacy that Blacks had contributed to America.

My experiences at E. P. Johnson established a firm foundation for my path forward in education. This remarkable structure, the first elementary school built for Blacks in Atlanta, provided what its students needed to achieve success. It was closed in the late 1950s, but my time there will always be remembered with great fondness and a sense of gratitude.

A TRIAD OF ATLANTA HIGH SCHOOLS:
HOWARD, WASHINGTON, AND TURNER

I graduated from E. P. Johnson as class valedictorian in 1948 and began high school at Howard High, joining my brother there. Howard High School was across town and outside of our school district.

Howard High was located in the Old Fourth Ward on Houston Street—now John Wesley Dobbs Avenue. It is currently being renovated to serve as a supplemental middle school for students in the Inman school district. Community organizers have insisted that Howard's legacy be preserved, and so it will still be called Howard Middle School. My father was friends with the principal, Mr. Charles L. Gideons. Though John and I were out of our school district, he allowed us to enroll. (Mr. Gideons and my father played golf together.)

I was enrolled at Howard High School for only one year. The school was named for a former slave, David T. Howard, who formed the first bank in Atlanta for Black people and donated the land for the original elementary school that preceded the high school. Several renowned Atlanta natives graduated from Howard: Rev. Martin Luther King Jr., the "father of civil rights"; Maynard Jackson, the first Black mayor of Atlanta; Walt Frazier, the famed NBA basketball star; Vernon Jordan, civil rights attorney; Lonnie King, leader of the Atlanta Student Movement; and Mildred McDaniel Singleton, an Olympic gold medalist in the 1950s.

My classes at Howard included English, math, citizenship, homemaking, and health. My first year in high school was very successful and I earned all As. I received an award certificate and the honor of having my name in the newspaper. The article lauded the A students of Howard High School.

But in November of my first year at this influential high school, my father died unexpectedly. I was twelve years of age and John was thirteen. We were heartbroken over the loss of our father. He had served as the head of the household, and it was difficult to lose him at our young ages. Mother was also deeply distraught over the death of her husband. She, however, managed the funeral arrangements and legal matters with her usual calm efficiency. She chose the Haugabrooks Funeral Home for the service. It was located on Auburn Avenue near the site of our former restaurant.

Even at the age of twelve, I could tell how despondent she felt. I could hear her crying at night. During the day, she tried to comfort and reassure us. The funeral was a blur for me. Mother allowed us to view our dad's body. The man in the casket didn't look like my father and I could not understand why he didn't. That viewing was a traumatizing event for me. To this day, I refuse to view bodies in caskets. I always want to remember people as I once knew them. At the cemetery, I was proud when an army officer presented my mom with a folded flag. Another officer played "Taps" on a bugle. Having served in the army during World War I and as a veteran, Dad received recognition from the military. As a child, I knew that he had served in the army, but I never heard him discuss what he did, where he was deployed, or how he was treated. He never discussed this phase of his life. As an adult, I realized that during World War I, the armed services were segregated. Black soldiers, though willing to fight for their country, received little respect for their efforts. The armed services remained segregated until 1948 when President Harry Truman used his executive powers to desegregate all branches of the armed services. My father died in November 1948—the same year when the armed services were desegregated. Unfortunately, he did not live to see this happen during his lifetime. This knowledge made me prouder of my father. He never discussed his problems in not receiving a full education and didn't live to experience a desegregated army. He saw no purpose in bringing these problems to his children. He wanted us to see and realize a more hopeful future. What an amazing father!

Dad's sister, Aunt Emma Joe Ward, came to live with us. She helped my mother receive friends at home after the funeral, and served food that was brought by family members and friends. I fled to my bedroom, fell upon the bed, and cried myself to sleep. That was my first funeral; I will never forget those feelings of pain and loss.

We had moved earlier that year to Kennedy Street. Our new home was located on the northwest side of town. Dad had purchased a grocery store with an adjoining house. The property included a rental house just around the corner on Griffin Street.

I vividly remember the purchase of that property. My father took me to the First National Bank to withdraw cash for the purchase. He placed it in a brown leather folder and gave it to me to hold while he drove. I was so impressed because I'd never held $8,500 in my hands before! We went to a lawyer's office to sign the contract and make the payment for the property.

When my father died, Mother was left to raise two children on her own. She also assumed management of the grocery store. Though her skills were not entrepreneurial, she persevered in this business venture through my college years and into my teaching career. She learned quickly how to keep the grocery shelves stocked and how to run a successful business. Aunt Joe helped her with sales, but Mom kept the business ledger. The rental house supplemented household income. Though we did not live a luxurious lifestyle, we never suffered from lack of what we needed. Mother made many sacrifices for her family as only a loving mother would. In looking through her papers, I discovered a business license that listed her race as Caucasian. The annual license was issued only after an inspector visited and inspected the store. I suppose the inspector thought that she was white instead of African American.

After our father's death, John and I were transferred to Washington High School, which was in our district. I was placed in 9L-1 based on my 4.0 GPA from Howard High. Classes ranged from 1 to 4. Students with the highest GPAs were placed in section 1 for each grade level.

I participated in the chorus but wanted to play in the band. Mr. Earl Starling, the band director, asked me to play the tuba because he found that I could read bass clef notation. I did not want to play such a large instrument, so I declined band participation. My dream was deferred once again. I wondered if I would ever achieve my childhood desire to participate in a band.

I did, however, participate in a special SSA, a three-part girls' sextet. Two sang first soprano, two sang second soprano, and two sang alto. Mrs. Elsie Foster Evans served as director. Our group was named the Sorors of Song. I sang second soprano and thoroughly enjoyed the challenge. We sang concerts at school, the YWCA, and at several local churches.

I liked my courses at Washington High. My favorite class was Latin. Mrs. E. Ross Robinson taught the class. She was an exceptional teacher and I embraced my first foreign language course with enthusiasm. I enjoyed it so much that I took four semesters of Latin during the ninth and tenth grades. Latin was the only foreign language course that I took during my high school days. Its foundation, however, helped me tremendously when I took French in college.

After two years at Washington High, I was transferred to the newly built Henry McNeal Turner High School. John was in his senior year at Washington High, and he was not transferred. We had never attended separate schools, and I missed walking to school with him.

Turner High, named for Henry McNeal Turner, was not as large as Washington High, but its modern architecture was fascinating. Turner was considered Atlanta Public Schools' elite high school: the teachers were all hand-picked. I loved the new high school with its attractive classrooms, excellent teachers, green and white colors, and new textbooks (for the first time in my years of schooling). Strangely enough, Turner High was listed as a Fulton County school for our first semester. My first report card is yellow, with Fulton County Schools printed at the top. The district lines were redrawn after the first semester and we received white Atlanta Public Schools report cards. We were then officially part of the Atlanta Public Schools.

On Founder's Day, I was inspired by a history of Henry McNeal Turner. The speaker related the interesting story of this outstanding African American after whom the school was named. He told us that Bishop Turner was one of the first Reconstruction officials elected in Georgia. After he was elected as one of the two Black Republican senators, they— along with the twenty-five elected Black congressmen—were expelled from the state legislature after serving only two months. All of the Black legislators were ousted by the white Democrats who held the majority votes. Henry McNeal Turner delivered a riveting speech to the white legislature. He told them that the Black legislators were elected by the Black citizens who had a right to be represented. Bishop Turner said that he had not come to beg, but that he came to "claim his rights as a man." Though Turner's appeal was denied, he was praised by Black citizens for his courage; his impact on organizing Blacks through both the church and politics would influence generations to come.

I learned much later, just before entering UGA, that the Rev. Henry McNeal Turner delivered this speech in 1868. Though he received some physical threats, it is amazing that he was not lynched. He was truly a man before his time. He was obviously not afraid to protest in the face of danger. I was proud that I was, in my own way, following in his footsteps. Bishop Turner's protest in 1868 took place well before the civil rights era of the 1950s and 1960s.

At Turner High School I was finally able to realize my dream of being in a band, playing the instrument of my choice: the clarinet. I proudly purchased a first-line Buffet clarinet with money from my savings, silently thanking my dad who started John and me on the path of an active savings account when we were very young.

As eleventh-graders, we were seniors twice for the eleventh and twelfth grades. No seniors transferred to Turner; only eleventh-graders and those in lower grades. A contest was announced for students to compose lyrics for the Turner High alma mater. Encouraged by the band director, I wrote a song and my lyrics were selected for Turner's school song. I was very proud, as was my mother. Though Turner is now closed, the alma mater is still sung at the annual Turner High Scholarship Breakfast, which attracts over a thousand alumni. Former Turner graduates from all over the nation attend this event and contribute scholarships to outstanding high school seniors. The alma mater song is the one thing that binds all classes together.

The two years at Turner passed swiftly as I reveled in my classes and in playing first clarinet in the band. Mr. B. Wayne Walton, band director, taught me to play the clarinet after school hours. I was an apt student and progressed very rapidly. My ability to read music stood me in good stead. Daily practice at home and at school produced great results. Though not an avid football fan, I enjoyed sitting on the 50-yard line and watching the games. The greatest joy for me, however, was when the band marched onto the field to perform the half-time show. We were encouraged by the cheers from our classmates, faculty, and family members.

I also resumed piano lessons in the eleventh grade. My new piano teacher, Mrs. Elsie Foster Evans, taught English at Turner High School, having been transferred from Washington High. I had participated in her Sorors of Song group at Washington High and she took a personal interest in me; we remained in contact for many years afterward.

My eleventh-grade classes at Turner included geometry, biology, English, social studies, band, homemaking, and physical education. I enjoyed most of the classes, but biology was not a favorite. Dissecting insects and small animals was not something that I wanted to do. Repulsed by this requirement, I solved that issue by asking my partner to do the dissecting; I would write up the reports. This plan worked perfectly, and I was able to earn an A for the class.

One class I particularly liked was the social studies class. It was called Problems of Democracy. After hearing informative lectures by our teacher, Mr. Brainard Burch, we were assigned to write a term paper. We were required to research a current topic relating to our segregated state government. I decided to write about the two-party system in Georgia. I knew that the county unit system was geared to disenfranchise larger cities like Atlanta or Savannah. Those cities were populated with more Black citizens. I wrote a letter to Governor Herman Talmadge to ask his views on the two-party and county unit systems. To my surprise and that of my teacher, I received a very extensive reply from Governor Talmadge. His lengthy reply praised the two-party county unit system. He did not address the inequities that allowed the white Democrats to retain power in Georgia. My term paper, however, did reflect how the unjust two-party system had empowered Democratic politicians for many years. Mr. Burch was so impressed with my term paper that he read it to the class. I was thrilled when my term paper earned a grade of A+. Though Governor Talmadge asked me to share a copy of my completed term paper, I did not. I knew that he would not have liked or agreed with my conclusions. It is quite possible that Governor Talmadge did not realize that Turner High was a Black school or that I was a Black student.

In my final year at Turner, I took English, geometry, chemistry, typing, business law, and band. I knew that I would need typing skills if I attended college. The daily timed typing tests frustrated me initially, but

I persisted until eventually I mastered the art of touch typing. That valuable skill remained with me throughout my entire life.

I enjoyed chemistry more than I had biology. The only problem was that I was not very careful when mixing the various chemicals. I burned my eyebrows off once when I emptied two volatile chemicals into the metal sink. The resulting combustion could have burned me badly. I, however, had the sense to jump away from the sink. I did like studying the periodic table and classification of elements. It was so enlightening to learn about the properties of ordinary items that we depend on and use in life: oxygen, hydrogen, water, plastics, and so on. The class sparked my interest in things that I had never thought about before. Those lessons resonate with me today, reminding me that I should not combine baking soda and vinegar.

Other activities also shaped my high school education. Though not athletically inclined, I joined the basketball team. I was cognizant of the fact that I needed to become well-rounded if I was to receive a college scholarship. I played guard on Turner's team for a brief period. At one game, I collided with a player on the opposite team and cut my inner lip. This injury put me out of commission in terms of playing my clarinet. Not surprisingly, the incident ended my basketball playing.

In my senior year, however, I joined the tennis team to, again, seek that elusive status of being well-rounded. I also wanted to earn a sports letter. This time, I was successful, and I did receive one. I treasure it even today. The accomplishment proves that I was not just a bookworm or nerd. I also learned many valuable lessons. At one school match, I was paired with a player from the opposite team who played as a left-hander. I watched her warm up and thought: "I can beat her easily." When the match began, I found it hard to determine just where her balls would land. I could not return balls that came from nowhere! I couldn't make the adjustment and she beat me at three games. My ego was shattered, and I was embarrassed. Coach Glover told me not to worry. She said that most players would have trouble with that type of unorthodox playing. She told me that I was overconfident. "You should have sought a solution while watching your opponent warm up," she counseled. I never made that mistake again.

I also participated in the drama club, an after-school activity. I was encouraged to join by my English teacher, Mrs. Beulah Tipton. We studied and produced several plays. The one that I remember most was *Arsenic and Old Lace*. Mrs. Tipton explained that this play was considered a black comedy for its gallows humor. She said that it was about the Brewster family who had descended from the people on the *Mayflower*. The play featured two spinster sisters who were insane. They took care of elderly men and poisoned them with elderberry wine laced with arsenic. When I heard the plot summary, I was immediately hooked. I liked mystery and intrigue. Mrs. Tipton assigned me the role of Martha, one of the maniacal sisters. After a month of intense rehearsals, we presented the play to a packed audience at Turner. The audience responded with robust laughter, clapping, and a standing ovation. We knew that we had a compelling drama! Mrs. Tipton decided that we would enter our play in a statewide drama competition. Turner High Drama Club won the competition with its confident acting.

My excellent grades earned me membership in the Honor Society, which meant a great deal to me and my aspirations to attend college. I was also elected vice president of the Student Council. But the most esteemed honor of my high school career was that of being chosen as student conductor of the band. I relished the joy of leading the band at football games. Leading my fellow students on such exciting occasions was what made me realize I wanted to teach band as my career choice.

When graduation time rolled around, I was named the class valedictorian and wrote a skit in lieu of a valedictory speech. The skit, presented at the graduation ceremony, was entitled *Setting Sails for the Future*. The production received a warm reception from the audience and was a lot more satisfying to present than a conventional speech.

I was so proud that I was a member of Turner High's first graduating class. I was also proud to receive the *Atlanta Journal* trophy as the most outstanding student in my graduating class. The *Atlanta Journal* newspaper published an article with a photo regarding this honor. When Mr. Davis, the principal, announced scholarship recipients, I was overjoyed that I was receiving scholarships from Clark College, Spelman

College, and Smith College. Tears filled my eyes as I realized that my mother wouldn't have to pay the cost of my college tuition and books. She was already paying for my brother's expenses at Howard University. I knew in my heart that the many honors had accrued because my parents taught us to always do our best, to believe in ourselves, and to be diligent and well-rounded in our school efforts.

I graduated from Turner High at the age of sixteen and turned seventeen later that month. My age at graduation, however, proved a stumbling block to one of my desires. Just prior to our graduation, seniors were transported to the Fulton County courthouse for voter registration. We knew the importance of voting, and I wanted to vote. I was initially told that I could not accompany my classmates on the trip to the courthouse. I protested that I was almost seventeen, and that I had earned the right to at least ride on the bus. My request was finally granted.

After the excitement of graduation, I reflected on the three high schools that I had attended. Howard High was named after a former slave who surmounted his former status. He worked hard, founded the first Black-owned bank in Atlanta, and became a philanthropist. Howard High started out as an elementary school.

Washington High was named after the legendary educator who founded Tuskegee Institute. His statue stands in front of this iconic school. The statue depicts Booker T. Washington "lifting the veil of ignorance" from his people. Washington High School opened in 1924 as the first public high school for Atlanta Blacks.

As noted earlier, Turner High's namesake, Henry McNeal Turner, served as one of the first Reconstructionist senators in Georgia. He also served as the first bishop of the African Methodist Episcopal Church.

These three high schools, with their rich history and legacy, educated me, inspired me, and challenged me to move forward to higher education. They, along with my parents, laid the foundation. Now it was time for me to follow in their footsteps.

CHAPTER THREE

On to Higher Education and My First Teaching Experiences

College was on the horizon and I received several scholarships, including one from Smith College in Massachusetts and one each from Spelman College and Clark College in Atlanta, now Clark Atlanta University. Although several of my Turner High classmates planned to attend Spelman, I could not make that choice. I had decided to major in music education so that I could receive teacher certification. Spelman offered a degree in music performance, but not in music education. I knew that Smith College was a prestigious institution but did not want to travel that far from home. I wanted to stay near my mother. I chose Clark because it did offer a degree in music education. Additionally, I chose Clark because my high school band director was an alumnus. He took me with him to rehearse with the college band while I was a Turner High senior. It had made me very proud to know that I could play well enough to handle college-level music while still in high school.

I liked the college band director at Clark College, Mr. Wayman A. Carver. Mr. Carver was a former jazz flutist who performed with the famous Chick Webb band and other renowned jazz ensembles. After a lengthy career in jazz performance in New York and other cities, he decided to return home and teach at Clark College. He left his jazz career because he felt that he could better support his family with a steady job in Atlanta where he resided. Mr. Carver served as the Clark College band director and taught instrumental courses. I took clarinet lessons from him and expanded my skills in playing. The Music Department chairman, Dr. J. deKoven Killingsworth, was from Menlo Park, California, and served as choral director of the Philharmonic Society. He also taught piano and the courses in music education. I took piano from Dr. Killingsworth and participated in the Philharmonic Society throughout my four years at Clark.

Another reason that I chose Clark College rather than Smith or Spelman was that they were both all-female institutions, and I preferred a co-ed education. I thought that I might be able to find a suitable husband at Clark College.

I embraced college life with a sense of true purpose. We had a week of freshman orientation where we were housed in a dormitory. This week was scheduled a full week before actual classes began, and included exciting days of meeting some of our professors; meetings of small focus groups designed to learn about college rules and regulations; tours of the campus to learn the various buildings and surrounding communities; placement tests to determine which courses we should take; and conferences with our chosen department heads. These serious gatherings were interspersed with fun-filled activities such as a freshman picnic on the grounds, an ice cream party in the dining hall, and nightly fireside chats in our assigned dormitories.

We spent the final evening at a convocation that can only be described as inspiring. Dr. James P. Brawley, president of Clark College, welcomed us to campus. The dean of women and dean of men spoke to us about our responsibilities as full-fledged college students. Outstanding alumni related stories of their days at Clark College and the exciting careers in which they were engaged. We had been told in our preparatory letters that the women should bring white dresses and the men, black suits to wear at the closing convocation. We stood in a huge circle around the auditorium and sang the Clark College school song, which we had learned during the week. The sight of the white dresses and black suits with white shirts enhanced by lighted candles held aloft as we sang brought tears to my eyes. I realized I was part of something very special that would affect me the rest of my life, something my own parents had never known.

Also, I kept a journal, and at the end of the week following this inspiring program, I wrote, as a seventeen-year-old freshman:

On Saturday evening of Freshman Orientation week, I mused as I walked back to my dorm: Thank God I am an American . . . an American who can go forward not as a Negro, but as a true American citizen to greater heights and to the pinnacle of success. Tonight, I pray a fervent prayer for the freshman class of Clark College, and the freshman classes all over the world—that they might dedicate themselves to the task of finishing this college course of four years, if possible, and then turn back to help their people who are not as fortunate as they—mold themselves into true citizens of the United States and of America so that someday the Negro race will not be called Negro and the Caucasian race called White, but all will be united together—in one race—the human race, having differences only in the pigment of their skin, texture of their hair, and having this in common—a citizen of the United States of America.

I kept that handwritten journal, and it is now housed among my papers in the Russell Library's Foot Soldier Project at the University of Georgia. Was this written statement (complete with run-on sentences) the beginning of my quest for equal rights and the end of the demeaning system of segregation?

I recalled that when I was in the ninth grade, Horace Ward, a graduate of Morehouse College and Atlanta University (later, Clark Atlanta University), and eventually Northwestern University Pritzker School of Law, had applied to the University of Georgia's law school and had been denied admittance. (He would go on to have a successful law career in Atlanta and was nominated by President Jimmy Carter to serve on the U.S. District Court for the Northern District of Georgia. He remained a federal judge for the rest of his career.) Even then I sensed a weariness and wariness of the "separate but equal" law that didn't prove true in our city that was labeled by Mayor William B. Hartsfield as "too busy to hate." Inspired by people like Ward, in a sense, my journey to UGA had already begun.

My freshman year at Clark was very successful, and I ended the year with a straight A record. As I continued in 1954, my sophomore year, the *Brown v. Board of Education* case ended with the Supreme Court ruling that public school segregation was unlawful. As college students, we received news of the decision with exuberance because most of us had attended segregated public schools. We wondered how long it would take for desegregated schools to become a reality. The ruling, however, gave us hope for the future of public education.

Because Clark College was a private Historically Black College and University (HBCU) institution, the ruling didn't affect us directly, but we certainly took note of the beginning of the end of segregation in public schools. Those hateful, incongruous walls in education were about to tumble down.

I continued my sojourn at Clark working as music librarian to supplement the academic scholarship. The music library was in a separate room next to Dr. Killingsworth's office and studio. Prof. Killingsworth, as we students called him, asked if I was interested in serving as the department's music librarian. With my past experience as a frequent patron of the Auburn Avenue Library, I readily agreed. The library's collection housed solely music-related materials. It included books, magazines, and journals. Prof. Killingsworth told me that I was to keep the books shelved properly, receive and shelve new books as they were purchased, and check out books to students. I would be paid $2 per hour and receive free dinners in the dining hall for my service. One must realize that the Robert Woodruff Library, which now serves Clark Atlanta University, Spelman College, Morehouse College, and the Interdenominational Theological Center, was not erected until 1982. The Music Department's library was the only resource for music students until that year.

I also participated in the college band and Philharmonic Society, which was Clark College's premier chorus, while applying myself academically. One highlight of the year was my induction into the Alpha Pi chapter of Alpha Kappa Alpha sorority. I was proud to be a part of the AKAs as we were called. Our chapter included top students at Clark and provided me with a sisterhood of friends that I enjoyed. I attended all meetings and in my senior year was elected to the position of Anti-Basileus (vice president). That organization was the only social group to which I belonged. My position as music librarian, the rehearsals for band and the Philharmonic (chorus), and practicing the piano and clarinet on a regular basis left little time for other social gatherings. I, of course, had lunch with friends after classes at the drugstore that was close to campus. It had a soda fountain and served burgers, hot dogs, and grilled cheese sandwiches. The Philharmonic rehearsed in the evenings. I would go to the dining hall for dinner with friends before rehearsals. The food was good, but I will never forget the "mystery meat" that was served quite often. After the Philharmonic rehearsal, I returned home on the bus to study and prepare for another day at college.

At one point that year Jeanette Reynolds, a junior, and I, a sophomore, were pictured in the *Christian Advocate* magazine as the most outstanding students at Clark College. The *Christian Advocate* was the official journal of the United Methodist Church. It was distributed to all Methodist organizations and institutions. Clark College was part of the Methodist Church. Interestingly enough, both of us graduated as valedictorians of our respective classes. More importantly, however, was the fact that during my second year of college (1954–1955) I reached the age of eighteen and was entitled to vote. And vote I did—and I have proudly voted each year since my sophomore year at Clark.

During my junior year, I was also named in the *Who's Who Among Students in American Universities and Colleges*; elected to the Alpha Kappa Mu Honor Society; participated in the Steering Committee for Freshman Orientation Week; served as secretary of the junior class; and traveled with the Philharmonic Society on a concert tour of Ohio during Clark's spring break. The bus trip to Ohio opened new vistas for me. We presented concerts in several Ohio cities. Snow was everywhere! As a true Southerner, I'd never seen so much snow.

At the time, the college's chorus members were divided into groups of four students. Each group was assigned to a private home for overnight stays. This was my first experience of living in a home with white people. Our Cleveland, Ohio, hosts were warm and friendly. Their hospitality also included delicious meals with the family, and I'll never forget the heating in their home. It was radiant heating in the floors and was a new experience for me because I never knew that such a thing existed. The cold weather and the whistling winds from nearby Lake Erie made this type of heating mandatory.

The weather in Ohio was freezing cold wherever we went, even in the majestic halls and churches where we sang. I well remember our concert in the famous Severance Hall in Cleveland, which hosts the Cleveland Orchestra in subscription concerts. I wondered how the musicians fared in this cold but beautiful and majestic concert venue. While the week-long trip was a wonderful experience, I vowed that I would never visit Ohio again in the winter.

Returning to school after the tour, I faced a heavy schedule of twenty hours of courses. My classes included several courses at the Atlanta University Library School because I had a second minor in library science. I was preparing for perhaps a career as a music librarian if music education didn't prove to represent a satisfying choice. Those courses were quite interesting as well as demanding.

As a rising senior, I decided to test my acquired skills in teaching music during the summer. I read about a position for a Muses (music) counselor at Camp Lenoloc in *Seventeen Magazine,* which I read on a regular basis. The magazine, aimed at an American teenage audience, was based in New York. I was nineteen years old and had read it for a long while. I applied for and was hired as a Muses counselor at the camp, which is in Bear Mountain, New York. Located only one hour from New York City, the camp was under the aegis of the West Orange YWCA in New Jersey. It was advertised as a typical camp with swimming, art activities, and all of the attractions that comprise summer camps. I didn't know anyone who had worked at this camp and had some difficulty in convincing my mother and Dr. Killingsworth (chair of the Clark Music Department) that I was mature enough for such a summer job. They finally relented and I was super excited about going to the New York area again.

My responsibility was that of general counselor for eight girls, and the organization and implementation of music activities for the camp. Lenoloc was structured in two four-week encampments for the hundred plus participating girls and counselors. I was assigned to cabin 11 with eight Jewish girls, all ten years of age.

To my surprise, in addition to playing "Taps" at bedtime, I was also tasked with playing a wake-up call at 7:00 a.m. to rouse the entire camp. I was given a battered bugle on which to play. How fortunate I was that I had taken a brass instruments class at Clark College the previous semester!

Although I was the only Black counselor that summer, I found it easy to interact and share experiences with the other counselors and camp director. Most of them came from the New York City area. It was so refreshing to get away from the segregated South and feel on equal footing with my camp colleagues. We were able to simply be friends, with a shared job of inspiring young people and helping them enjoy the outdoors. I learned much about working successfully with people of other races. It was enlightening as well as fulfilling.

That summer I embraced the camp work routine and organized music classes for the campers. I also led evening camp song sessions, coordinated an all-camp presentation of *Peter Pan*, and took my eight Jewish campers across the lake each week to attend Friday evening synagogue services. I also learned to enjoy lox and bagels, marinated fish, potato latkes, and other Jewish foods at the receptions that followed the services. On Sundays I played a small pump organ for outdoor church services that were organized for the Christian campers and counselors.

A CITY GIRL DISCOVERS THE GREAT OUTDOORS

Though not an outdoors person, I learned to relish the beauty of nature that the camp offered. Lenoloc was situated on a brilliant blue lake and was bordered by a verdant forest. We were in close company with a variety of wildlife: deer, raccoons, otters, snakes, and bears. This was, after all, Bear Mountain with an elevation of over 1,800 feet.

All counselors were required to pass a swimming test and learn how to handle a canoe—including righting an overturned canoe. We also learned how to secure life jackets for our campers. They were requisites when counselors rowed campers across the lake. Initially, I was very concerned about how my hair would fare with this much exposure to water. Before leaving home, however, I was able to have my hair treated to a permanent. This worked perfectly and lasted through the eight weeks of camp.

One incident that frightened me happened during a visit with campers to the nearby forest rangers' headquarters at a state park. Two of the rangers described the various types of snakes that were found in the forest. One ranger showed the campers some poisonous snakes—and then some nonpoisonous ones. He then demonstrated how to hold a snake and allowed some campers to touch it. Unaware that I was quite afraid of snakes, he handed the snake to me. As the reptile coiled itself around my arm, I almost fainted. I held the snake's head so tightly, I almost strangled it! The ranger quickly retrieved the snake and I breathed a sigh of relief. I told him afterward (out of my campers' hearing) to ask counselors if they were afraid of snakes before handing one over.

That was not my only unpleasant encounter with snakes. Fran, the nature and pioneering counselor, and I took my eight campers on a walk through the forest. Fran told the girls that when approaching a log, they should look at the log, and then step over it. One should never step on a log as snakes often take refuge beneath logs. Fran led the way and demonstrated stopping to look and then stepping over a log. The girls followed and did as they were told. I followed the eight girls. When I reached the log, a copperhead snake emerged, its head ready to strike. I froze and called out to Fran. She always carried a small hatchet in her belt. She saw the situation, threw the hatchet, and severed the snake's head. The campers applauded Fran's quick action. I ran to Fran and gave her a bear hug. Always ready to teach a lesson, Fran told the girls that I had done the correct thing in freezing my movement. Little did I know that when I agreed to be a camp counselor and teach music, I would also be a naturalist.

The camp counselors took turns enjoying a night off. On one occasion, I rode with four other counselors to New York for a one-night break from our duties. We went to a bar. They each ordered a drink. I had never drunk alcohol before because I was underage. They insisted that I take a sip from their drinks. This I did. I sipped vodka, gin and tonic, a whiskey sour, and beer. Afterward, I felt dizzy and disoriented but didn't tell my companions. I tried to join in their lively conversation, but soon told them that I was sleepy. We left the bar and started the long drive back to the camp. When we arrived, I had a quick trip to the bathroom and regurgitated over and over. I'd never felt so sick before. I don't think that the other counselors meant to make me ill; they had no idea that I was not accustomed to drinking alcohol. I blamed myself for my naiveté. That type of incident never happened again in my life. Looking back, I realize now that I not only was able to test my skills in teaching music that summer, I also learned some valuable life lessons.

FINISHING UP AT CLARK COLLEGE

My senior year at Clark College was just as busy with many experiences that prepared me for a promising career. I served as student director of the Clark College marching and concert bands and directed one of my original compositions at the annual spring concert. I continued my job as music librarian for the Music Department.

That year I was assigned to my former high school (Turner High) for student teaching. There I met Charlayne Hunter and Hamilton Holmes as high school students. Little did we know then that our paths would cross five years later as the first three African Americans to integrate the University of Georgia.

I met Charlayne when she asked to interview me regarding my writing the Turner High alma mater. She worked as the editor of the Turner High *Green Light*, the school newspaper. I also learned that year that Hamilton was a top-notch student academically as well as a star football player on Turner's team. (We had in common the fact that both of us graduated from Turner as valedictorian of our classes.) I had not met Hamilton in person but since I was doing my student teaching during the fall semester, football games were the talk of the school. Teachers in the teachers' lounge often spoke about Hamilton, his prowess on the football team, and his academic excellence. I wasn't surprised when I heard, before I left student teaching at Turner, that he was the candidate for the honor of valedictorian.

As student teacher, I observed both instrumental and choral classes. After two weeks of observation, I took control of the classes in both disciplines. My notes for my observations and conferences with both the band and choral directors proved invaluable when I took over the classes. The advanced band and chorus were preparing for their spring concerts and I enjoyed working with the students to help them toward that goal. I felt so fortunate that I had the opportunity to work with

Mr. B. Wayne Walton who had started me on the path to my chosen career. He was apparently pleased with my work because I received top grades from both supervising teachers for student teaching. Dr. Killingsworth congratulated me for working in both band and choral student teaching. After doing the student teaching, I concentrated on completing the remaining courses at Clark College successfully. Because I was working toward a dual minor, I once again took twenty hours of courses that spring.

My senior recital that year featured me playing both the piano and clarinet. But Dr. Killingsworth, department chairman, did not approve of my desire to teach band. He said that women were better suited as choral directors. While I respected his right to his opinion, it did not deter me from pursuing what I'd decided to do. I told him: "Perhaps I could teach both choral and instrumental music." I reminded him that I had participated in Clark's Philharmonic Society for four years and incorporated both band and chorus in my student teaching. Though the women's rights movement in America was almost nonexistent in 1957, I was determined to follow my personal choice in teaching. When I discussed this decision with my mother, she encouraged me to follow my dream. Fortunately, her unfailing support provided me the confidence that I sought and I was able to respectfully defy the department chairman.

I graduated once again as class valedictorian. I had majored in music education and minored in secondary education and library science. I felt ready to assume my career as a music educator.

MY FIRST TEACHING JOB, THEN ON TO GRADUATE STUDIES

Though I received several job offers, I accepted a teaching position at John Hope Elementary School, where Mr. Ralph A. Long was principal. I chose John Hope because it was in the Old Fourth Ward near the area where my family's restaurant had been located. I had learned earlier that Mr. Long, a Clark alumnus, operated a strong school environment. I also learned that Mr. Long was a quiet supporter of civil rights and social justice. After being interviewed by him and observing the school in operation, I was convinced that John Hope should be my choice. I never regretted that decision.

I taught fifth grade initially, along with band and chorus after school. Though my preparation at Clark did not include how to serve as a regular classroom teacher, I felt that I could do a creditable job with fifth-graders. Mr. Long promised that I would teach only music the following year. I also thought that I could do the legwork in developing a band from scratch. I would have to recruit students; purchase the larger instruments; organize a band parents' organization; invite instrument companies to come and explain to parents how to rent the smaller instruments, and so on. The chorus would be easier to organize because nothing was needed except talented singers. I did this with both groups after school.

In my second year of teaching, I was able to drop the fifth-grade class assignment and serve as full-time music teacher or music specialist. This job was perfect for me. Here, I was able to concentrate on what I loved the most and was best at: imbuing my students with the love of music. Though the salary was not great (I was receiving approximately $3,600 a year), it was rewarding to see the students grow in musicianship and in their appreciation for music.

Fortunately, Mr. Long also valued music education and gave me exceptional support. I developed a fifty-voice elementary chorus and a forty-piece elementary band. I also taught general music to all classes K–7. The challenge of teaching each grade level required careful planning to keep the students engaged. I quickly learned that the attention span of kindergarteners and first- and second-graders was drastically shorter than that of older students. I could teach them the basics of music—melody, rhythm, harmony, and form—but with different approaches. I utilized music listening with each grade level but with selections that were age-appropriate. Singing, playing rhythm instruments, and movement activities kept the students active along with the listening lessons.

John Hope Elementary's student population numbered approximately five hundred students. Each class received one thirty-minute lesson per week. My teaching schedule included seven classes per day with band and chorus included. The band and chorus met on alternate days with their schedules alternating each week. Few people realize that music specialists have no "down time" or seat work. Classes are scheduled with only a five-minute break between groups. The music teacher must prepare the materials—music textbooks, recordings, instruments, and so forth—for each class with little time between. It is an exhausting but fulfilling job.

One of the enrichment experiences that we offered our students was a trip to the City Auditorium to hear the Atlanta Symphony Orchestra (ASO) in concert. Of course, Young People's Concerts for schools were segregated. White students were scheduled for a morning concert and African American students attended in the afternoon. I took a group of fifth-, sixth-, and seventh-graders to the concert in my second year of teaching. We entered the auditorium and sat in eager anticipation of hearing symphonic music.

The opening selection was always a patriotic song with audience participation. And while I consider myself a patriotic person (born on Flag Day) and love my country, sometimes the choice of songs was inappropriate. At the time, Maestro Henry Sopkin served as conductor of the ASO. He asked the audience to stand, turned to the orchestra, and began conducting the song's introduction. When I realized that the orchestra was playing "Dixie," I instructed my students to sit and not sing. They obeyed. When the large audience of children and teachers saw that we had sat down, they followed suit. Henry Sopkin turned around when he didn't hear any singing and then continued conducting the song to its end. I believe that he understood why our students refused to sing "Dixie." This was one of those moments in my life when I was able to make a powerful statement and engage my students in a "teachable moment" without having to show anger. I simply asked my students to join me in the respectful protest, and our statement paid off. Future concerts didn't include the playing and singing of "Dixie." The orchestra played "America," "America the Beautiful," or "The Star-Spangled Banner."

That event reminds me of a similar incident. Mr. Long brought a large box of paperback music books to my classroom. He told me that the State Department had sent the music books to supplement our outdated music textbooks. I eagerly opened one of the books and saw that the first song was "Dixie." The facing page included a drawing of "pickaninny" Black children in the field picking cotton. I told Mr. Long that I could not use these books with our students. He immediately understood and asked what I wanted to do with the books. I suggested that we burn the entire box of books on the dirt-packed playground. That we did!

The song "Dixie" was written by Daniel Emmett and was used as the rallying cry of the Confederacy. It was, therefore, very offensive to most Blacks, and that sentiment continues even today. Beyond being a song, it is an emblem of the era of enslaved people in America and romanticizes the horrors of the times. As an educator I can see the need for keeping our society aware of its power, but I could never present this kind of thing to my young students as an admired or respected piece of music devoid of cultural implications.

INTERLOCHEN AND MY FIRST TASTE OF GRADUATE STUDIES

During the summer of 1958, I began graduate study toward the master's degree in music education at Interlochen, Michigan, a highly respected summer music camp. Founded in 1928 in northwestern Michigan, Interlochen included a division of the University of Michigan and graduate-level courses were offered to those seeking postbaccalaureate study.

At that time, the state of Georgia was awarding grant-in-aid stipends to African American teachers to do graduate study in northern and midwestern states. The state did this so that Black teachers would not attempt to attend the all-white University of Georgia. This ploy was designed to keep UGA segregated, but three years later, that status would change. I chose the University of Michigan because its music program was among the most prestigious in the nation.

Mildred Burse, an orchestra teacher at Turner High School, accompanied me to Interlochen. My former band director, B. Wayne Walton, had shared with her the fact that I was going to Interlochen. Mildred and I found that we were the only African Americans enrolled in the University Division in 1958. Our experiences there turned out to be life changing, a delightful and inspiring summer. I took music courses and participated in the University Band and Chorus. I heard and performed more music than I had experienced in my entire lifetime. Music was being performed all day and evening by the Junior, Intermediate, High School, and University performance groups.

Each concert concluded with a theme from Howard Hanson's *Romantic Symphony*. I can still hear the ethereal strains wafting through the trees in the outdoor performance hall. That beautiful music continues to bring tears to my eyes as I remember the summer of 1958.

Interlochen has changed to a year-round academy for talented young artists. It no longer offers University of Michigan graduate courses, but the summer programs have expanded to include visual arts, theater, film, dance, and creative writing, in addition to music.

The next two summers (1959 and 1960) I spent on the University of Michigan's campus in Ann Arbor. I loved UM with its imposing buildings, spacious campus, and beautifully manicured grounds.

The music education courses that I took were interesting and stimulating. I had great respect for the wonderful professors and their high-quality instruction. I especially liked the course Practicum in Teaching Elementary Music. The professor presented several strategies or potential lessons for teaching music and then asked the class members to create similar strategies. Class members took turns in presenting their strategies or lessons. This course proved very helpful to me when I returned to John Hope and taught my students. I looked forward to returning in the summer of 1961, but that was not to be.

CHAPTER FOUR

1961: Integrating the University
of Georgia's Graduate School

During my fourth year of teaching at John Hope, I went home on the evening of January 11, 1961, and watched the nightly news with my mother. We saw the telecast of an ugly riot that was happening at UGA. It was taking place in front of Center Myers, Charlayne Hunter's dorm on the campus.

I had followed Charlayne's and Hamilton's court case as they sought admittance to the University of Georgia as the first two Black undergraduates. For 175 years, our state university, the oldest land-grant institution in the nation, had been segregated. The governor at the time, Ernest Vandiver, had proclaimed in his election campaign: "No, not one" Negro would integrate a Georgia public school. This was our governor, the man meant to represent and lead the people of Georgia. His misguided sentiment chilled me to the bone.

The Georgia state legislature had even passed a law that would deny funds and close any public school that integrated. The segregationists were continuing to defy the Supreme Court's 1954 ruling in *Brown v. Board of Education of Topeka*, which declared state laws establishing separate public schools for Black and white students to be unconstitutional. The arch segregationists, including UGA's president, O. C. Aderhold, had agreed with Vandiver's pledge. Now, after eighteen months of litigation and repeated refusals to admit the students, federal court judge W. A. Bootle ruled in favor of the admission of these two Black students. Sadly, they entered the campus to large groups of students yelling "Two, four, six, eight—we don't want to integrate!"

Charlayne and Hamilton began classes, however, with no further overt actions from the student body. But on the evening of January 11,

UGA had just lost a basketball game to its archrival, Georgia Tech, and emotions spilled over into school life from the sport competition. The students, already angry over the admission of Charlayne and Hamilton, flooded Lumpkin Street just outside of Center Myers dorm where Charlayne was housed. They yelled racial epithets, hurled rocks at Charlayne's windows, and were generally out of control. The rioters also included some local adults and members of the Ku Klux Klan.

Dean of Students J. A. Williams finally called on the state troopers to come and quell the riot. Though positioned on the periphery of the campus, the state troopers refused to help, saying that they only took orders from Governor Vandiver. Appeals were also made to the Athens police. They, too, refused to help, arriving after the riot was essentially over. It was the dauntless dean of men, William Tate, who waded through the huge crowd collecting student IDs, and who was finally able to obtain control of the unruly students.

Charlayne and Hamilton were suspended from campus "for their own safety and the safety of other students." (This maneuver was reminiscent of the time when Autherine Lucy was suspended and ultimately expelled from the University of Alabama's campus. Autherine Lucy applied to the University of Alabama as a graduate student. She was finally admitted in 1956 but was suspended after an angry mob threatened her safety. Afterward, Autherine was expelled on the basis that her lawyers had made derogatory remarks regarding the university.)

As my mother and I watched the telecast in horror, I made a decision: I would assist these two brave students in their efforts to integrate our state university by transferring from the University of Michigan to the University of Georgia. When I shared this thought with my mother, she was decidedly opposed to my transferring to UGA. She said that it was far too dangerous to even contemplate going to the campus. She pointed out the riot that we had just witnessed. In this moment she also told me—for the *first time*—about four Blacks who were brutally murdered in Monroe, her hometown, in 1946. Two Black couples, Roger and Dorothy Malcolm and George and Mae Dorsey, were shot to death by an armed, unmasked mob of white men. They were retaliating against a physical altercation between Roger Malcolm and a white man named

Barnett Hester, who had molested Roger Malcolm's wife. The two couples were driving back to the Malcolms' sharecropper home after bailing Roger out of jail. The car was stopped by the angry, heavily armed mob. The men and then their wives were pulled from the car and taken to a spot near the bridge. They were bound together and then shot sixty times by the white mob. Black and white spectators witnessed the vicious murders. Though the onlookers knew the mob participants, no one was ever tried or convicted for the crime and none of the spectators talked about it. They were too afraid. The crime is known as the Moore's Ford Bridge lynching.

Undaunted by what my mother had just related, I looked at her and said: "Mother, this is something that I just *have* to do. That horrible crime that you have just described happened when I was ten years of age. Hopefully, it will never happen again. The injustices that we endure every day won't stop until we do something about them. This is something that I can and want to do."

When she saw my resolve, she reluctantly agreed to support me in this decision.

A RISING TIDE OF REVOLT AGAINST INJUSTICE

The early 1960s ushered in the beginning of the student movement in Atlanta. It began on the heels of the student movement in Greensboro, North Carolina. Students from the Atlanta University Center, inspired by the Greensboro movement and tired of the injustices of the Jim Crow laws that permeated the city, were organizing and implementing sit-ins at lunch counters and picketing at department stores, movies, restaurants, and other public facilities.

The Atlanta student movement was led by Lonnie King, Julian Bond, and other brave and visionary students. The older Black leaders pleaded for a slower pace of integration. The students from Morehouse College, Spelman College, Clark College, Morris Brown College, Atlanta University, and the Interdenominational Theological Center, however, wanted integration of everything—and wanted it immediately. They were relentless in their organized protests against the discriminatory system that prevailed. Many were jailed for their actions, but they simply started over and were often jailed many times.

I wanted to assist the students in this struggle for social justice but knew that I couldn't. As a public school teacher and an employee of the state, I would have been fired. But that evening, I realized what I *could* do to help in this struggle for civil and human rights. I could transfer from the University of Michigan to the University of Georgia. I felt that I couldn't just stand on the sidelines and watch: I had to actively participate. Though a rather quiet person, I felt strongly—like Gandhi and Dr. Martin Luther King Jr.—that we must be the change that we want to see in the world. I felt that even as one person in this disturbing world of Jim Crow laws, I could contribute to the cause of civil rights and social justice. I could do this by asserting my rights as a citizen and integrate the University of Georgia's Graduate School. This gesture was both a symbolic and a pragmatic one, one that I thought could have a lasting effect. My mother and I had a very special and close bond. It was supremely important that I receive her blessing and approval. When I received it that night, I felt so relieved.

The following Monday morning, I shared the decision with my principal, Mr. Long. He was a "behind the scenes" civil rights activist and readily embraced my plan. I was overjoyed. He advised me to contact Mr. Jesse Hill Jr., another activist who had been among the Atlanta leaders who recruited Charlayne Hunter and Hamilton Holmes to challenge the university's system of segregation. Hill was an astute businessman and civil rights supporter who was president and CEO of the Atlanta Life Insurance Company for almost twenty years (1973–1992) and the first African American to be elected president of a major city's Chamber of Commerce.

I met with Mr. Hill and he shared the hurdles that Black students had to overcome for admittance to UGA. I sent a letter to the UGA Graduate School and requested an application for admission to the 1961 summer session. I received the application forms in three days and set about completing them.

Mr. Hill walked me through the admission requirements and together we made sure I proceeded correctly and with detailed care. Signatures from two UGA alumni were required but I could ignore that because Judge Boyd Sloan had ruled it unconstitutional in January 1959. Other requirements included a visit to the Fulton County courthouse to have the court judge verify that I was a model citizen. College/university transcripts had to be sent along with a brief biography and a trip to Athens for a personal interview with the registrar, Walter N. Danner.

I made a list of these requirements and checked them off as they were completed. I requested that transcripts from the University of Michigan and Clark College be sent to UGA. Mr. Hill accompanied me to the Fulton County courthouse. The clerk of the court, rather than the judge, signed the application form. I completed the remainder of the application and mailed it to UGA.

One might wonder about the rationale for such careful adherence to following admission requirements. After Horace Ward's attempts to enter UGA's Law School and the three applicants to the Georgia College of Business (now Georgia State University), the state of Georgia wanted to prevent future desegregation attempts. University officials, Georgia legislators, and the Board of Regents decided to formulate new admission requirements. The segregationists were determined to continue defying the Supreme Court's 1954 ruling. New requirements included personality tests, character assessments, and an age limit for college/university admissions. The legislators passed a bill stipulating that no student over the age of 25 would be admitted—with the proviso of exceptions for white applicants. This last barrier to integration caused concern for higher education administrators because they felt that this strategy could weaken enrollments along with their operating budgets. I didn't want my application to be found lacking in any way, so I followed Jesse Hill's instructions to the letter.

I did not try to hide the fact that I was a Negro applicant. In fact, on my application form, I listed my membership in the NAACP and the names of my high school and college. My answer to the question of why I wanted to attend the University of Georgia was also a huge clue. I wrote:

Attending summer school is no new experience for me. I have done summer study for each of the summers I have been out of college. The summer of 1958, I studied at the National Music Camp at Interlochen, whose University Division is a branch of the University of Michigan. The summers of 1959 and 1960, I did serious study toward the M.E.E. degree in music education at the Ann Arbor campus of the University of Michigan. Despite the fact that I received state aid for my summer studies in Michigan, I spent far more money than I would have to spend as a student at the University of Georgia. Of paramount importance to my decision to apply to UGA is the fact that it is very close to my home, Atlanta. I see no reason why I should journey several hundred miles to Michigan when I can pursue the same studies at UGA. I am a resident of Georgia, have lived here all of my life, am teaching here, and therefore feel that I am entitled to study here if I can meet the necessary qualifications.

That rather forceful declaration must have given someone pause because I received a letter that requested a copy of my high school transcript. This request, in addition to the transcripts for college and university, is usually not required. I smiled as I complied with this request. I knew that my high school grades were even better than those of my college and university.

Thus I began a lengthy wait of five months before I was admitted as the first Black graduate student and the third Black student to enter the hallowed halls of UGA.

ACCEPTED BUT NOT WELCOME AT UGA

Before I actually entered, news articles appeared in the *Atlanta Journal* and the *Constitution* about my possible admission. I was working for the *Atlanta Inquirer*, a militant Black newspaper, as its music editor. The *Inquirer* published several articles about my application to UGA. One article stated that my admission would represent a victory for Black teachers in Georgia because they would be eligible to enroll at UGA rather than travel to northern or midwestern states for advanced study.

Remembering that one of the requirements was a personal interview with the registrar (I hadn't been invited to campus for the interview), I boldly wrote letters to Registrar Walter Danner and to graduate school dean Gerald Huff informing them that I would visit the campus during our school system's spring break for interviews. I then scheduled the interviews with Mr. Danner and Dean Huff.

Jesse Hill drove me to Athens for the interviews. The interview with Dean Huff was very pleasant. He was friendly and encouraging about my potential admittance.

The interview with Mr. Danner and his assistant, Paul Kea, however, was quite unpleasant. I was asked if I had ever visited a house of prostitution. I responded in the negative, telling them that I was a teacher, a professional, and had no reason or desire to visit a house of prostitution. This question still rings in my head as an utterly disingenuous and insulting attempt to undermine my self-esteem and dignity. Mr. Danner then told me that UGA might not accept my credits from the University of Michigan, and that I would lose all of that time and money. My immediate thought was: "UGA might not accept credits from one of the top ten universities in the nation?" That thought, however, remained unspoken.

I told him that I would never lose what I had already learned, and that I still wanted to attend UGA. Even as a twenty-four-year-old, I realized that Mr. Danner might be hoping that I would become confrontational in response to some of his questions and comments. Having read the account of how Danner had characterized Hamilton Holmes's interview responses as "evasive" and "inconsistent," I wanted to maintain my composure and not give him or Mr. Kea any indication of disrespect from me. Though I succeeded in remaining calm, I left the interview feeling very disconcerted, but still determined to follow through on my quest for admission. It is the nature of insults and slights that they can crawl into our psyches and poison our self-worth; what these men tried to do to me was unconscionable, and I am glad I was able to focus my energy on the higher purpose, which was to make UGA a place for *all* Georgians.

Though I didn't know it at the time, an eleven-page FBI-style investigative report was done on me to see if there were flaws in my character and lifestyle that would allow UGA to deny my admission. This report, supposedly done by the Georgia Bureau of Investigation, sought to find out if I had shoplifted, been arrested, used drugs, had a venereal disease, had an illegitimate child, and so on, which would be comical if it wasn't so denigrating and inappropriate. In addition to investigating me and my background, they also investigated my entire family. After finding nothing that would support their denial of entrance, I received my letter of admission barely a month before I was to begin summer study in Athens.

The unwillingness of state politicians to admit me was published in an *Atlanta Journal* article just before I received the admittance letter. The article stated:

> A high level conference was held at the capital last week at which officials reluctantly decided that Miss Early would have to be accepted for admission. It was felt that in view of her good scholastic and teaching records, to reject her would be to invite an order from U.S. District Judge W. A. Bootle to admit her and maybe a contempt of court citation, too, for violating the injunction. (*Atlanta Journal*, May 10, 1961)

When I read that article, I realized that Georgia's political leaders did not want a repeat of the negative publicity that our state received following the January riot. The media—local, state, national, and international—had not applauded the outrageous riot and those who had supported Charlayne's and Hamilton's suspension. Our state and its flagship university were, instead, severely criticized. Governor Ernest Vandiver had hastily convened the Georgia legislature to repeal the law that called for a closure of public schools that desegregated. He wanted to avoid further damage to the reputation of the state and its university.

I wouldn't be welcome, but my acceptance was something that the politicians felt they had to approve. Appearances on the national stage trumped the deep prejudices of local men of power for a moment. After all, 1961 was a year of many societal upheavals: The Freedom Riders began their tour of the South, the Berlin Wall started going up in Germany, and the Soviet Union put a man in outer space, which instigated a rush of scientific aspirations. Was it possible my local effort to integrate a state institution as a music educator would become part of the fabric of this new world?

I received my letter of admission on May 10, 1961. I was out of the city when the letter arrived at home. Mr. Long had asked me to serve as coordinator of a week-long camping experience (outdoor education) for 100 of our elementary school students. The camp was located at Lake Allatoona. It had rained for the entire week, and I was constantly challenged in keeping the students and counselors engaged in interesting activities. We were boarding a bus for a tour of the Allatoona dam when I was called back to the camp office. There was a call from the Graduate School dean, Gerald Huff, informing me that my application for admission to the University of Georgia had been approved. Words cannot express my unbounded elation as I heard this news. I had passed the first hurdle and didn't know what to expect next, but I was in! A new journey was about to begin.

The news media had received the confirmation before me, and several articles appeared in the local newspapers. It was old news by the time I returned home from camp but I still felt thrilled that my decision and the university's acceptance were both discussed in the public press. What *was* news was the coverage of how the Freedom Riders were being brutally attacked by the Ku Klux Klan in Alabama and other southern states.

The Freedom Riders were comprised of Blacks and whites who were challenging the South's refusal to comply with court-ordered desegregation of interstate travel. Despite the brutal attacks on the brave Freedom Riders, they continued their travel throughout the southern states. I read of these violent confrontations and wondered if this statement of white supremacy would spill over into Athens and UGA when I registered a few weeks later. I didn't, however, spend any sleepless nights worrying about this. I was determined to follow through with my plans. I refused to be intimidated by those who might not agree with my right to attend the university. I trusted in God for guidance and protection.

I was entering UGA five months after Charlayne and Hamilton had been admitted. Since they were returning to Atlanta with other plans for the summer, I would be the lone Black student on campus during the summer of 1961. How would this feel? What would it mean to my fellow Turner High students? My education?

No more riots had occurred after the infamous January incident, but the university students were still making it clear that Black students were not welcome on campus. A printed PROCLAMATION that was apparently widely distributed among students read:

We, the student body of the University of Georgia, fully deplore and resent the court-ordered intrusion of two Negroes into this century-old white institution. It is more than obvious that these people are not here to secure an education as they assert, but to further the social scheme of those who would destroy the most basic of all freedoms—the freedom of association. The courts have illegally usurped the power of the state and the school officials to deal with this matter. It is up to us to save the university from destruction. While we disavow the use of violence in any form, we hereby pledge ourselves to the use of the ultimate weapon so widely and effectively used by these people—the weapon of 'passive resistance.' We will NOT welcome these intruders. We will NOT associate with them. We will NOT associate with white students who welcome them. We love our school. We Will save it.

This undated manifesto, currently housed in the Russell Library, is signed "Students for Passive Resistance."

I was not aware that this document existed until the year 2000, and I'm glad that I wasn't. It illuminates, however, the hardened attitudes of some of UGA's students toward African American students during those first few years. It set a pattern of ostracism and hostility that permeated the campus for a very long while. And the irony that they were using passive resistance as espoused by Dr. Martin Luther King Jr. was especially gnawing.

Federal troopers had accompanied Charlayne and Hamilton to and from classes for the first few weeks. Since no additional overt violence occurred, the troopers left the campus. The negative attitudes of the majority of UGA's students, however, did not abandon the campus. They prevailed, but so did the determination of the first three African American students.

MY ARRIVAL AND FIRST IMPRESSIONS
OF UGA AND ATHENS

My high school band director, B. Wayne Walton, drove me to UGA on June 12, 1961. As we rolled down the highway toward Athens, B. Wayne said, "You're very quiet. Are you afraid?" I replied, "No, I'm not afraid, just curious about what reception I will receive." Arrangements had been made to have a graduate student (May March) accompany me to registration. Before she arrived, a white, male law student came to Dr. J. Arthur Kelly's office to welcome me to UGA.

Dr. Kelly was a local Black dentist who also had an office in Atlanta. When he heard that I was going to attend UGA, he visited me at my home to talk about Athens and his involvement in the community. He graciously agreed to allow me to use his office as a meeting place.

The young law student—I do not recall his name—and I chatted for a few minutes, and then I received a call from May March saying that we should wait until later that morning so that the registration lines wouldn't be too lengthy. The law student, B. Wayne, and I decided to go to Killian's restaurant on Broad Street for breakfast (Dr. Kelly's suggestion). Killian's was one of the few Black restaurants in Athens at that time. (The Killian home, located next to the restaurant, hosted Hamilton Holmes during his terms at UGA.) B. Wayne drove, and we received many curious stares as we proceeded to the restaurant. We were greeted warmly by Mrs. Ruth Killian, the family's matriarch. We had a delicious breakfast with lively conversation.

When we returned to Dr. Kelly's office, May March arrived. May was a white graduate student from North Carolina. She was completing her master's degree in art that summer. We bonded immediately. She told me that she needed to stop by the Fine Arts building on North Campus first so that she could retrieve her summer catalog. I was happy that she needed to go there first because I didn't know where the Fine Arts building was located. Each of my classes would be held there. Leaving Fine Arts, we chatted on the way to Stegman Gymnasium, which at the time was located at the bottom of the hill where Baxter Street and Lumpkin Street intersect. As we approached the long line that snaked into the gym, the students who had been talking loudly as we approached suddenly stopped talking and stared at us. Their complete silence was deafening. We ignored them and continued to talk softly to each other as we joined the line.

Once inside the gym, May and I had to separate because we were in different fields. I found the Music Department desk and was warmly welcomed by the music professors who were handling the registration.

After completing my selection of courses, I met May again for a trip to the Academic Building (now the Holmes/Hunter Building near the Arch) to pay our tuition and get room assignments. I was amused to find that they didn't have a room card for me. I wondered if they thought that I wasn't coming, or if I'd decided to room off campus. After a lengthy wait, I was finally assigned to the same room in Center Myers (a freshman dorm) that Charlayne had occupied.

I walked back to Dr. Kelly's office and B. Wayne drove me to Center Myers. We were met by the housemother, Mrs. Minnie Porter, as she led us to the assigned room. She was affable and friendly, and told me that I'd need an electric fan in my room (no air conditioning in the dorm at that time). B. Wayne took my luggage to the room and then we went to the local Colonial grocery store to purchase some food supplies. Returning to the dorm, B. Wayne helped me to unpack groceries, gave me a big hug, and left to drive back to Atlanta.

A wave of loneliness swept over me as I realized that I was alone on a generally unfriendly campus. I thought to myself: "This is what you wanted to do! Get over it!" I marveled at the friendliness shown by the law student, May March, and Mrs. Porter. I thought: "Maybe it won't be so bad after all."

I set about unpacking my clothing and making my bed. Afterward, I was so exhausted, both emotionally and physically, that I immediately fell asleep on my newly made bed.

I awoke in the early evening and realized that I'd overslept a previously scheduled dinner engagement with Dr. Kelly. I made a sandwich and surveyed my new surroundings. The room was not a regular dorm room. It had originally been used as a counselor's suite and then as an office for one of the campus sororities. The bedroom included a metal chest of drawers, a single bed, a desk, and a tiny closet. There was a small bathroom with shower and tub, a small kitchenette, and an adjoining room that was locked. The authorities had hoped that Charlayne—and then I—would opt to prepare our meals in the room and not use the dining hall or cafeteria. Looking at the kitchenette I thought: "I won't be using that very often because I didn't come here to cook!" The bathroom was convenient so that we didn't have to share the facilities used by the white students. That was impossible anyway because the actual dorm rooms were upstairs, far removed from this suite on the ground floor.

The first morning of classes demonstrated just how isolated I was. I had chosen to wear a dress that had a back zipper. I needed someone to help me to zip it up. I had to go across the lobby area and ask Mrs. Porter to zip my dress. In those days, female students didn't wear the shorts and jeans that are commonly worn on campus today. Dresses and skirts were *de rigueur* attire.

DAILY LIFE ON CAMPUS AS A NEW GRADUATE STUDENT

The day was bright and beautiful; the fragrance of the flowers that I passed lifted my spirits. As I walked from the dorm to my first class, I smiled and said "Good morning" to those I met along the way. Not a single person smiled back or responded.

I walked up the hill to the Fine Arts Building, a very imposing white-columned hall, where all of my classes were located. I panicked because the room where Advanced Music History was to be held had been changed. I ran back upstairs to the Music Library and asked the librarian to assist me in finding my class. Mrs. Dunaway, the librarian, readily agreed with a smile. Her sunny personality helped to dispel the sting of the snubs I'd received earlier from students.

Dr. Mitchell, the professor, greeted me with a smile and welcomed me to the university. He was smoking a pungent old pipe and the scent reminded me of my father, who had also smoked a pipe occasionally.

I felt relieved and comfortable until other students began to arrive. I was once again given the cold shoulder as the students chose seats as far away from me as possible. I had thought that graduate students would be more accepting of my presence because they were more mature and perhaps more worldly than the undergraduates. I was mistaken. They kept their distance and most didn't even acknowledge my presence.

While at UGA, I often felt as if I was invisible. Dr. Mitchell didn't seem to be aware of the students' hostile attitudes. I noticed that my other professors also ignored the students' unfriendliness. I felt uncomfortable because after all, we were all music educators, and we were in the classes to grow professionally. Also, I had been up North in numerous classes with other students and the energy had been thrilling; I knew that it was possible to have positive, exciting, shared experiences in the classroom. But the classroom atmosphere at the University of Georgia that summer felt so tense that I was tempted to burst out in singing "Getting to Know You" (from the Broadway musical *The King and I*). Of course, I did not do this because I knew that the students wouldn't understand my motives; not even a sense of humor appeared to be a way out of this uptight, apprehensive environment.

I had studied Music History at Clark College, but it was more of an introductory course. In the Advanced Music History class at UGA, we studied various music eras: Renaissance, Baroque, Classical, Romantic, and post-Romantic. This Advanced Music History course included frequent analysis of the music with comparisons of the various composers and more in-depth discussions of the times in which they lived. Fortunately, the attitudes of some of my fellow students changed after the first exam.

My second day on campus ended with another troubling incident. I was scheduled to take the Graduate Record Examination (GRE). In their attempts to find damaging information about my background and character, university officials had neglected to check whether I'd passed the GRE. It was required for UGA graduate students.

I had received a letter that required me to take this exam on my second day on campus. May March had sent me a note advising me to get plenty of sleep before the exam, and to just relax while taking it. I did this but was still apprehensive. Would I pass? The University of Michigan hadn't required the GRE, so I'd had no experience with this difficult exam.

That morning, I walked to the Ag auditorium where the exam was being administered. The room was crowded with other graduate students who had to take the GRE. I sat down in a seat that was close to the entrance, and immediately the students who were sitting in that row got up and moved to other rows. That was not a very good start to taking an important exam. I was both insulted and crestfallen. As it turned out,

I did pass the GRE with flying colors but I really had to focus on the questions because the incident greatly affected my inner psyche.

My third day on campus was my twenty-fifth birthday. I felt even more despondent over the continuing cold reception of students and the fact that I had no one with whom to celebrate my quarter of a century birthday. As it turned out, I did indeed have people who cared.

When I returned to the dorm after classes, Mrs. Porter told me that I'd received a call from May March inviting me to the Presbyterian Student Center at 6:00 p.m. for hot dogs. Dr. James E. Popovich, a speech professor who had sent me a letter of welcome before I came to campus, was to escort me to the center. I told Mrs. Porter that I definitely *was* interested in this kind invitation and she called Dr. Popovich to confirm my acceptance.

He came at 6:00 p.m. and escorted me to the student center. There, I met Hardin "Corky" King, the Presbyterian campus minister, his wife, Mary Lisle, and their adorable twin daughters. After a warm welcome, I was taken to the spacious backyard where I found May March and two other Presbyterian students. They had planned a birthday party for me! I don't know how they knew that this was my birthday. We had hot dogs, hamburgers, fries, ice cream, and a decorated cake. I was overwhelmed with this wonderful and unexpected surprise. To this day, that's the most special birthday that I've experienced in eighty-three years. Tears of joy streamed down my cheeks as I realized that these wonderful people, who didn't even know me, cared.

When the party ended, Dr. Popovich took me on a brief tour of the campus. I was not familiar with the campus except for the Fine Arts Building, the Academic Building, the library, Snelling Dining Hall, and Stegman Gymnasium. As we approached the dorm, I expressed my gratitude for his kindness and thoughtfulness. He told me that I could call upon him for any questions or problems. When I returned to the dorm, I gave a huge slice of my birthday cake to Mrs. Porter. So ended my truly memorable twenty-fifth birthday.

The real problem that I faced—and knew that Charlayne and Hamilton faced daily—was that we never knew what to expect. Some days were rather normal; others were days when I felt like a pariah because of the ostracism or the racial taunts. I tried to take each day in stride and to depend upon God's guidance. I also kept in my heart the idea that I was improving my skills as a teacher of music, a universal language that had no boundaries.

The next day I went to Snelling Cafeteria for lunch for the first time. I always ate alone because no one else was friendly enough to invite me to have lunch or dinner with them. When I entered the cafeteria, some students began making catcalls. When I got into the cafeteria line, other students began throwing lemon slices from their iced tea glasses. Several slices struck me, and they didn't stop until one landed in a serving container. The cafeteria manager came out and asked that the students stop. I was so angry and insulted over the incident that I found it difficult to eat my lunch.

Afterward, I told Corky King, the Presbyterian minister, that I wouldn't return to the cafeteria—that I would just eat in my room. He told me that this was just what they wanted and that I should return. He and his wife, Mary Lisle, accompanied me to the cafeteria for lunch on the following day. No catcalls and no lemon slices were thrown.

I continued to eat at the cafeteria for lunch and most dinners. I never had to worry about a place to sit. If I approached a table with a vacant seat, those already sitting would get up and find other seats.

When I tired of this blatant hostility, I would go to Killian's restaurant for dinner. The food was always delicious, and the friendly company of Mrs. Ruth Killian and her family was a breath of fresh air. Killian's represented my "go-to" refuge, or home away from home when I needed a break from the ostracism.

I had thought that I could handle any situation at UGA. I was, after all, twenty-five years of age and self-selected. No one had asked me to attend UGA. Transferring there was *my* choice, but I was human, and the slights and troubling incidents really got under my skin at times.

I brought my new, white Ford Falcon car back to campus after the first week of classes. Of course, B. Wayne had come to drive me back to Atlanta at the end of the first week. I looked forward to weekends in Atlanta where I had family and friends with whom to talk and have fun. I've always been a loquacious person; probably talked too much, but

I was gregarious. I didn't share the unpleasant incidents that happened on campus with my mother because I knew that she worried about me. I didn't want to upset her further. I did, however, share the surprise birthday party with her, and she was very pleased.

That year I began attending Ebenezer Baptist Church on my weekends at home so that I could hear the riveting sermons preached by the young Dr. Martin Luther King Jr. He had come to Atlanta to co-pastor Ebenezer with his father. Dr. King's messages about nonviolence and love for all people were both inspiring and thought-provoking. I was in awe of this brilliant young minister. His sermons gave me the strength and courage that I needed to deal with the tenor of the times at UGA. His sermons encouraged me to "let go and let God" guide me.

Listening to Dr. King's melodious voice quote scriptures such as "Let justice roll down like the waters and righteousness as a mighty stream" stirred me in the depths of my soul. He would then relate, in simple terminology, how this theme embraced his philosophy of love and nonviolence. I felt a deep kinship with his sense of how to survive and succeed in my own challenging world at the University of Georgia.

GETTING DOWN TO THE WORK
OF GRADUATE STUDIES

I remember an impending first exam in Advanced Music History. It was originally scheduled to be administered just before the Fourth of July weekend. Several students implored Dr. Mitchell to postpone the exam until after the holiday. I wanted to get it done before the Fourth so that I could enjoy Independence Day. Dr. Mitchell decided to accept the majority opinion.

After the holiday, we got a taste of how inclusive our exams would probably be. That first exam was very comprehensive and rather difficult because it was an essay exam rather than multiple-choice. I had studied hard, knew the answers, and really enjoyed responding to the questions.

When Dr. Mitchell returned our papers, he announced that I had the highest grade on the exam—an A. I could tell that my classmates were astonished. After that exam, a few of them began conversing with me during class, but never outside of class. Perhaps this was the first crack in the disrespectful wall. I thought: That's what we must do—we have to prove to the world that Blacks *can* compete favorably in terms of academic achievement. One of the popular theories at the time as to why Blacks should not be admitted to "white" colleges and universities was that they were mentally incapable of competing in an academic environment. Well, that theory was blown to oblivion—at least in my Advanced Music History class.

In addition, Hamilton Holmes had already demonstrated his scholastic excellence during his first two quarters at UGA. Some students were upset with him for setting the curve so high on tests and exams. Significantly, Hamilton would prove his academic acumen by being inducted into Phi Beta Kappa at UGA.

Dr. Mitchell gave us some very difficult assignments. I remember one where we were assigned to research some ancient Latin music manuscripts. I went to the main library that evening to begin my research. As I approached the steps of the library, a group of young men spread themselves across the top steps as though to block my entrance. One of them said: "I smell a dog." Another said: "That's not a dog, that's a [n-word]." I was hurt and humiliated but continued to walk toward the steps. I decided that I would be the bulldog that I was supposed to be—and barge through their barrier if necessary. Just as I neared the top step, they broke ranks and laughed loudly. I proceeded into the library, but I didn't get much research done that evening. I was too upset. I was eventually able to get my research done on the following day. I continued to visit the library, but never experienced this troubling situation again. Again, I thought how ironic it was that here at an institution of higher learning—in fact, at the library—I was faced with ignorance and stupidity.

I really liked my second class: Advanced Music Theory. The professor, Dr. John Anderson, was friendly and made music theory (usually a dull course) come alive. It was an interesting but demanding class. In teaching mixed or unusual meters, Dr. Anderson used a recording of "Take Five," composed by Paul Desmond and made famous by Dave Brubeck, written in 5/4 meter. He had us stamp on the counts of one and two and clap on the one, two, three beats.

In general, that first summer I found that the UGA Music Department professors were kind and fair. The department served as a place of refuge during my first quarters on campus—despite the unfriendliness of many fellow students. I appreciated the unbiased attitudes of my professors and feel sure that their example helped shape some of my fellow students into more sensitive, mature human beings. I hope so. I continued to drive back to Atlanta on weekends when I didn't have assignments that required library work. One weekend, however, I went home with a troubled heart. Despite my resolve to practice nonviolence, I had erred.

On the previous weekend, I was walking to the post office to post a letter to my mom. I had written to tell her that I had library work to do, and that I would see her on the following weekend. Today's students wouldn't understand because they would have just used their cell phones or emailed their mother. In 1961, however, cell phones didn't exist. Neither did iPads or personal computers. Indeed, we had to use electric or manual typewriters for written reports. And there was no phone in my dorm room; I had to request use of the housemother's phone for calls. That option provided no privacy and I used her phone only in emergencies.

A group of young male students were on the opposite side of the street as I walked to the post office. They saw me and began yelling racial epithets. I ignored them and continued walking. They began to throw small rocks at me. I ignored this too until one rock struck me on the cheek just beneath my glasses. I was so irate that I picked up a rock and threw it back at them. Of course, I didn't hit anyone, and they ran away laughing.

I attended Dr. King's church on the following Sunday and spoke to him after the service. I told him about the encounter and said that I regretted that I had not used the nonviolent strategy in response to the students' harassment. While I was not badly hurt physically by this action, I nevertheless saw it as symbolic of a mean-spirited and vicious reaction of these white students to a fellow human being. Dr. King laughed and told me not to worry; he would have done the same thing that I did. I didn't believe him but felt relieved. It's difficult to avoid retaliation in situations like that, but—we should at least try. In some ways, when faced with violence, it's hard not to retreat into a visceral response of self-preservation. I was not proud of my behavior, but Dr. King reminded me that I was also human.

Vocal Problems was my third course that summer. Dr. Ray Leonard taught the class and seemed rather uncomfortable with my presence. I later discovered that my initial impression of him was inaccurate. He had a German accent and was obviously a professional singer as well as a voice professor.

I was surprised when he invited me to participate in the summer chorus. This was a noncredit activity and considered an extracurricular class. I accepted his invitation to join the chorus and thus became the first to integrate extracurricular activities at UGA. Charlayne, with her experience in journalism at the high school level and internship at the Louisville *Times*, tried, during her senior year at UGA, to work on the *Red and Black* student newspaper. She, however, was not pleased with the menial assignments given to her and she quit the newspaper rather quickly.

Hamilton, known as the star football player on Turner High's team, wanted to play at UGA but he was not allowed to do so because it was felt that his participation would be too dangerous for him. My sense is that he ended up concentrating on his school work and occasionally enjoying a pickup game of basketball with neighbors in Athens, rather than participating in any official extracurricular activities or sports.

MUSIC AS A SOLACE AND INSPIRATION

So, in the summer of 1961, I tested the waters of an extracurricular class. All music majors feel the need to actively participate in music making, even if they are not performance majors. At the first rehearsal, the young woman who was to share a music folder with me declined to do so. Though we stood side by side, she would stand well in front of me and I couldn't see the music. I sat down and was asked why I was sitting. I told Dr. Leonard that I could not see the music. He instructed the music librarian to give me a separate folder. And so, my fellow second-soprano and I were the only chorus members who had individual music folders. I guess she felt that sharing a folder would place her too close.

Though I would have preferred playing in the band (there was no summer band), I did enjoy singing in the chorus. It gave me a much-needed outlet and release from the constant studying and stress. It also reminded me of the power of music to help us transcend our earthly challenges. I could sing my way out of despondency and frustration.

Dr. Leonard prepared the chorus for a summer concert to be held at the UGA Chapel. I was selected as one of the singers in a women's sextet. This small ensemble was to sing one of Johannes Brahms's love songs.

I was very proud and wanted to invite my mother, brother, and a few friends to attend the concert. I also wanted them to see the majestic UGA Chapel with its classical Greek architecture, huge Doric columns, and gigantic oil painting of *St. Peter in Rome*. The chapel, built in 1832, is one of the most beautiful buildings on campus, in my opinion. Like music, its architecture reminds us of the human ability to transcend everyday human frailty.

I must have shared my intention with someone because I was told by Dr. Leonard that I could not invite guests; the university was only integrated for Charlayne, Hamilton, and me. I was stunned. I had assumed that Charlayne, Hamilton, and I had the same rights and privileges as any other students.

When I protested this not-so-subtle discrimination, I was told to request a conference with the dean of students. As it happened, I couldn't get a conference with him until after the concert was over.

Donald Hollowell had served as the chief counsel for Charlayne and Hamilton during their court trials. He had contacted me before I left for UGA to say that I could call him if I experienced any difficulties. As a schoolteacher, I didn't have the money to pay an attorney. Mr. Hollowell generously offered his services gratis. When I contacted him regarding this problem, he told me that he would call Dean Williams. Hollowell called me back to say that the university was taking this stance because it could not ensure the safety of my family and friends in traveling to and from Athens. Attorney Hollowell also told me that he didn't feel that this was a good idea. He thought that this would represent a potential danger for family and friends. I accepted his advice because I certainly did not want to place my mother, brother, or friends in any danger. It simply had not occurred to me that attendance by others at an evening concert would present a danger. I felt certain that white students wouldn't perceive this as a problem for their friends and family. But Blacks, in 1961, might experience problems.

Donald Hollowell served as friend and counselor many times during my stay at UGA. We remained in close contact even after I had graduated. I will never forget his wonderful friendship, sage advice, and assistance.

Though I felt that this situation was unfair, I thought as I stood on the stage with the chorus and then with the women's sextet: "Well, at least, there's one African American singer on this stage." I also hoped that one day this type of situation would no longer exist. And today, thanks to the civil rights movement, it does not.

I remembered, too, that though my mother's family lived close by in Monroe, I never visited them on my trips to Athens or back to Atlanta. I realized that they had to live and work in Monroe—and I didn't want my decision to attend UGA to cause problems for them.

I will, however, always be indebted to Dr. Leonard for having the courage to invite me to participate in the 1961 summer chorus. It represented a growth experience for me, for the other chorus members, and for the university.

At the end of the summer, despite the recurring problems and a few vexing roadblocks, I had excelled academically. My advisor, Dr. M. J. Newman, was so pleased with my progress that he asked me to consider taking a leave of absence from my teaching job and return to UGA for the spring and summer sessions of 1962. He said that I could possibly complete my master's degree by the end of that summer.

I returned to Atlanta happy and satisfied that I had survived, enjoyed my classes, and had dispelled, at least for some students, the myth that Blacks could not compete academically.

CHAPTER FIVE

Back to Work . . . and a
Historic Graduation at UGA

I resumed my music specialist position at John Hope Elementary School in Atlanta with pleasure and anticipation. I was looking forward to working with my students once again because teaching was so rewarding; after all, they were my main motivation.

After reflecting on Dr. Newman's suggestion, I talked with Mr. Long, my principal, about a possible leave of absence to continue my studies at UGA. He thought that this was a splendid idea and said that he would hold my position at John Hope until I returned. He advised me again to talk with Jesse Hill regarding the leave of absence.

I talked with my mother first and told her that I would have to take a leap of faith because I would have no salary or insurance coverage after the fall semester if I took a leave of absence. I was concerned about household expenses because she was only receiving Social Security. Most of the household bills were paid by me. She told me that she was supporting me in this venture, and that she would be okay. My fraternal aunt, Emma Joe Ward, lived with us and my mother planned to ask her to assume more of the household expenses.

I then discussed the leave of absence with Jesse Hill. He, too, approved of this plan and said that he would explore avenues of financial assistance. And so that fall I wrote a letter to the Atlanta Public Schools requesting a leave of absence for spring through summer of 1962. The leave was approved.

Soon afterward, I heard from Dr. Horace Tate. He was the executive secretary of the GTEA, the Black Georgia Teacher Education Association. (The two state professional teacher associations were segregated in 1961.) The GEA or "white" teacher association remained all-white until 1969.

Dr. Tate told me that he was initiating a support fund among the Black teachers in Georgia including the Atlanta-based Gate City Teacher Association. He was asking teachers from both professional organizations to contribute $2 each to assist my return to UGA so that I could complete my degree. He felt that all Georgia's Black teachers would benefit from my successful graduation because it would open the doors of UGA to them. Dr. Tate was a veteran of university integration. He was the first African American to receive a doctorate from the University of Kentucky, and he knew how crucial these first steps were to the progress of Black educators everywhere. The *Atlanta Inquirer* began publishing articles about my return to UGA for the spring/summer quarters.

Once this process started, it was gratifying and reassuring to see support coming from so many entities. Pretty soon, the Black Georgia teachers who had been asked to contribute to a support fund had generously contributed over one thousand dollars. The Gate City Teacher Association comprised of Black Atlanta teachers also made a sizable contribution. My church, Mt. Vernon Baptist, the John Hope PTA and fellow teachers at John Hope Elementary, and other civic organizations also made sizable contributions. Before leaving to return to UGA for the spring quarter I had over two thousand dollars to pay tuition, room and board, and miscellaneous expenses.

I had conflicting feelings about this generosity from so many people. I had always been able to manage my own expenses, but I realized that this time I needed help. It was a humbling situation.

MORAL SUPPORT AS IMPORTANT AS FINANCIAL SUPPORT

I soon realized that many people were concerned about my safety in what they still perceived as a hostile university. In addition to the financial gifts, I received a protection pendant from Father Edward Banks of

St. Paul of the Cross Catholic Church; a small Bible from Margaret Davis Bowens (inscribed with "Keep this with you at all times"); and a carved *Praying Hands* plaque from the Wataushi Club. These spiritual gifts comforted me on my journey more than the donors would ever know.

Father Banks told me that he was ordained as a priest in the year that I was born and that this created a special bond between us. He admired the courage of those of us who were at UGA and wanted me to know that he would always pray for our safety. He remained a friend and confidante long after my years at UGA.

Margaret Davis Bowens was Andrew Young's school principal in New Orleans. She moved to Atlanta when her husband was appointed as a professor at Atlanta University. She was president of the Alphabettes, the wives of members of Alpha Phi Alpha fraternity. Under her coordination, the Alphabettes honored me at a program just before I returned to UGA. The organization presented me with a check and she gave me the small Bible, which I still have today.

Another boost I got was from my friends and colleagues at the Wataushi Club, a civic club of which I was a member and which was comprised of several of my friends. They feted me with an elaborate banquet and program at Paschal's restaurant.

With this exceptional support from so many people, I felt ready to return to my studies at UGA. I have always felt that none of us can truly be successful without the support of others as well as the all-abiding love and grace of God. As Dr. Martin Luther King Jr. once said: "The time is always right to do what is right." I felt that my path—my journey—was indeed right at that time.

Shortly before my return, I read in the *Atlanta Inquirer* that another graduate music student, Marybelle Warner, had been admitted for the spring quarter. The article was entitled "Now There Are Four." She was the wife of Dr. Clinton Warner who was Charlayne's and my primary physician. Marybelle Warner did not reside on campus; she commuted to and from Athens on the days when she had classes. We never met because our class schedules were different. She did not pursue a degree; she just attended classes in the spring and summer of

1962. I think that her husband, a civil rights activist as well as a noted physician, encouraged her attendance to support Charlayne, Hamilton, and me. The two of them (Marybelle and Clinton Warner) were pioneers of civil rights in other ways. Dr. Warner was the first African American to purchase and move into a home in the previously segregated Cascade Heights subdivision in Atlanta. Marybelle Warner later enrolled at Georgia State University and became one of its first Black graduates.

With these kinds of people as inspiration and an abundance of support from family, other friends, and even people I did not know, I realized that I could *not* disappoint them; I *had* to succeed in my goal of receiving the master of music education degree at UGA.

BACK IN ATHENS

Upon my arrival in Athens that spring, I registered and went to the Academic Building to pay tuition and receive my housing assignment. I was reassigned to the freshman dorm, Center Myers. I was to room with Charlayne because they had opened the adjoining room in the suite.

Charlayne and I were both disappointed. She was a junior and I was a graduate student. We both wanted to be housed in dorms with students near our own ages. The administration, however, was determined to keep us isolated as much as possible. Center Myers represented the ideal choice for that isolation. We both mused: "When will they begin treating us like regular students?"

Charlayne and I got along as roommates, though I was over five years her senior. On one occasion, we decided to eat dinner at the restaurant at the Continuing Education center. We overheard a woman who told her companion that she was moving to another graduate dorm because they had several available rooms. Char and I wondered: "How dumb do they think we are?" We'd been told that there were no other available rooms at the university. (Hamilton Holmes was continuing to live off-campus with the Killian family.)

Another time, when Charlayne and I had dinner at the Continuing

Education restaurant, a service officer (I think that he was Navy) was sitting at a table just across from us. After we were seated by the hostess, the man beckoned a waitress and asked if the restaurant was part of the university. She told him that it was, and he asked to be seated at another table away from us. I guess that he was too close for comfort. I was reminded of my father's service to our country and disappointed in this man's lack of respect for his fellow Americans.

Charlayne kept her door open in our small suite and we chatted at times but didn't talk much about the problems that we faced on campus. There didn't seem to be much to gain by discussing unpleasant incidents and, besides, it was hard enough to endure them, so why not use our time in the dorm for a chance to recharge our emotional batteries?

One of the things that we did discuss was that of our driving back to Atlanta. We both owned white cars. This was a pure coincidence. Charlayne said that she had heard campus gossip that the NAACP had purchased the white cars for us. When asked why Hamilton's car was blue, a student told the group that the NAACP purchased a different color for males! Though it probably was true, I didn't think that this was very comical because I had the bill of sale that proved that I'd purchased my own car. In fact, I never received any financial assistance from the NAACP.

We both had noticed that whenever we left campus to drive back to Atlanta, a light blue car always followed us. It turned around when it reached the Clarke County line. We later learned that this was the state patrol following us. They were under instructions to protect us while we were in Clarke County. Beyond the county line, we were on our own. That bit of information sent chills down my spine. Were we really in danger?

In 1964, when I began my educational specialist degree, I discovered that there really was a potential for danger in driving to and from Athens.

As the semester progressed, we were still isolated at the dorm. If we went into the lobby to watch the evening news on television, the girls there would stop talking and some would just leave the room. They let us know in subtle ways that we were not welcome. But one night,

Charlayne and I heard a knock at the door. When I opened the door, three girls were standing there. They asked if they could enter. We invited them in and they began to talk. One said that they really wanted to get to know us and that they were glad that we were at UGA. Another said that they were rushing a sorority and that the pledges had been warned against befriending us. If they were discovered talking with us, they would be dropped from the sorority's pledges. I told them that we certainly understood and that they should stay away. We would not want to be the reason that they weren't accepted into their chosen sorority. They left, and I wondered about the entrenched racism that still existed on UGA's campus. Would it ever end? It seemed to be a kind of sleeping dragon, and every so often, it would awaken and breathe toxic fiery breath into all our lives.

For the first time, my spring semester courses included some classes that were outside of the department of music. I was assigned to a social studies course: Personality and Social Adjustment. When I went to the first class, the professor asked all the students to just stand around the wall. He then began assigning seats alphabetically by last names. I noticed that he skipped my name when he got to the Es. The last student to be seated had the name of Zachary. The professor instructed me to sit behind him. I said: "But my last name begins with an 'E.'" He responded: "You'll sit where I tell you to sit." I replied that I wouldn't sit in the last seat and left the classroom. I immediately went to the Dean of Students' office to report the incident. Nothing was said of the unprofessional attitude of the professor. I was simply assigned to another section of the class that was taught by a different professor. I thought: "Not much has changed since last summer. Now, it's a professor, ostensibly an expert on 'social adjustment' but not very enlightened or understanding." I don't remember the name of the first professor or the second. I erased the memory of both because the incident was just too painful. It reminded me that I was still on a generally unfriendly campus. It was obvious that some students and professors were still entrenched in their belief that Black students were not acceptable.

My other nonmusic courses included Guidance and Exceptional Children. Fortunately, I had no problems with those classes and earned grades of A in both. Conversely, I earned a grade of B+ in the social studies class.

The spring semester passed quickly, and I relished the thought that I was in the home stretch. I had met with my adviser during the winter quarter to decide on the title of my research paper or special project. This was an alternative to a thesis, but the requirements were much the same. I had submitted a tentative outline and after approval, begun the research. I had decided to do a comparative study of the major music textbook series. The comparisons were done in terms of their content: authenticity of included folk songs, patriotic songs, song material from other cultures, quality of the teacher manuals, and so forth. Dr. Newman was very helpful in guiding me through the various requirements for this major project.

I was simultaneously taking my last few courses—one of which was not in music. I had Instrumental Music Techniques and Instrumental Music Materials. The out-of-area course was Speech for Elementary Teachers taught by Dr. James E. Popovich. He was the person who had written me a letter of welcome before I came to campus in 1961 and who also took me to the surprise birthday party at the Presbyterian Student Center. We had remained in touch during the previous summer and the spring quarter.

When I returned to campus in March, he took me to lunch at the Dairy Queen on Broad Street. As we approached the outside window to order, an elderly Black woman walked up to me and said, "Honey, we have to go around to the back to order." I told her that I appreciated her advice. She shook her head and walked around to the back.

The woman who was taking orders looked or rather glared at Dr. Popovich because she realized that he was ordering for both of us. If looks could have killed, he would have been dead. He calmly ordered burgers, fries, and drinks for the two of us. We sat down at one of the outside tables to eat. We, of course, were the object of many stares. I was a bit amused while feeling impressed at Dr. Popovich's courage. He was defying the city's code of conduct in ordering for both of us and dining with me out in the open and on a busy street.

One must remember that though the university was integrated, the city of Athens was still very segregated. While I was in Athens, there were few social outlets for Blacks, at least not in the heart of town. No restaurants—except for Killian's—bars, movies, or the like were open to Blacks. There was a clear dividing line between Black and white citizens. The only Blacks on campus were those who were enrolled: Charlayne, Hamilton, Marybelle, and me. There were no Black professors until 1968 (after I'd completed my second degree) when Dr. Richard Graham was hired as a professor of music. Any other Blacks on campus held service jobs as maids, janitors, or cooks. The Athens public school system was still segregated and this wouldn't change for several years.

Dr. Popovich's class was quite intriguing because we studied plays and creative writing for elementary students, as well as how to teach speech writing and public speaking to students. We were required to keep an organized notebook with class notes, class projects, corrected tests and exams, and so on. I made certain that my notebook was well organized, attractive, and in good shape throughout the course. I received a grade of A+ on the notebook, the final exam, and the course itself. I will always be appreciative of Dr. Popovich's friendship as well as his mentoring and concern for me while I was attending UGA. I found out later that he had allegedly been encouraged to leave UGA shortly after my graduation. I don't know if this was because of his liberalism or some other cause, but I do know he was a great help to me and my career and well-being at UGA.

While taking my last three courses, I typed my special project/thesis on onionskin paper, had it bound, and submitted it to my adviser. After his approval, I had to meet with a Music Department committee to defend my work. Everything was in order. My project was accepted, and I was ready for graduation.

During that summer of 1962, I was delighted with the fact that there were two additional Black graduate students in music: Mattie Jo Arnold and Alice Martin. I knew both of them. Alice Martin was a talented pianist who had attended Washington High in Atlanta. I don't know where she attended college. She was Alice Idlett when I knew her, but had married and was now Alice Martin. Mattie Jo Sims Arnold had attended Clark College. She was in my Elementary Music Education class that I taught one summer at Clark College. (Marybelle Warner was continuing her studies from the spring quarter.) We didn't have any classes together because they were just beginning and I was near the end of my course work. Sadly, neither continued their study through to a degree. Despite our extremely busy schedules, Alice and I attended two concerts and often had meals together. It was so much fun to have someone with whom to chat while dining.

Four other Atlanta Public Schools teachers were on campus attending summer workshops: Fredericka Hurley, Charles Gaines, C. P. Griggs, and Juanita Long. It was so encouraging to have nine Black students on UGA's campus that summer. That was certainly a miniscule percentage of the total student body but it was a big improvement over three students, and I had the sense that things were slowly changing for the better.

Charlayne was there also and we continued as roommates. I have often been asked if Charlayne and I are still in close contact with each other. The answer is no. Charlayne, by her own admission, was very taciturn in her demeanor. I suppose that it was partly because of our age difference and partly because we were in different fields. She was an undergraduate in journalism and I was a graduate student in music education. We did have meals together occasionally, and once attended a movie (the only Black movie theater in Athens at that time). We did not, however, engage in deep or highly personal conversation while in the "Black suite." We were both too busy with our studies.

Later, after we had both graduated, I saw and spoke to her at the funerals of Hamilton Holmes and Donald Hollowell. We saw each other at the fortieth anniversary of UGA's desegregation in 2001, and again at the fiftieth anniversary in 2011. I was also invited to attend the School of Journalism's DiGamma Awards ceremony in 2007 when Charlayne received its Distinguished Achievement in Broadcasting award. At that occasion, we were photographed, and it is one of the two photos that I have of us together. Taking photos when we were roommates at Center Myers dorm was furthest from our minds. We were basically in survival mode at that time. In November 2015, I attended the Atlanta Press Club's Hall of Fame celebration at the Intercontinental Hotel.

Charlayne Hunter-Gault and Hank Klibanoff (the 2013 Mary Frances Early Lecture speaker and Pulitzer Prize–winning journalist) were honored along with journalists Dennis O'Hayer and Dick Pettys. I had the opportunity to personally congratulate Charlayne and take the photo with her and her son. I also congratulated Hank Klibanoff—a personal hero of mine.

After I had completed my courses and passed the oral defense, I prepared to leave UGA's campus. I went home before returning for the graduation. The Russell Library has a photo of me in the "Black suite" sitting on my blue suitcase holding clothes that I was taking back home. Mattie Jo Arnold and Alice Martin had come to assist me in packing my belongings for the last time. One of them took the photo, the only one that I have of me in the "Black suite." I took one of them sitting at my desk eating lunch. Both of these photographs are simple clues to a complicated past. The originals are part of my archives at the Russell Library at UGA, which I donated to UGA's Foot Soldier Project in 2012.

What a carefree feeling I had driving back to Atlanta after completing all requirements for the master's degree in music education! It was truly exhilarating to realize that I had attained my goal. In addition, I had also done well academically, receiving all As during the last quarter.

Moreover, I was going to have the distinction of becoming the first African American to receive a degree from the University of Georgia. That was not the reason I had come, but it felt so rewarding to realize that I had done my part to assist in bringing about equality and social justice in the state of Georgia. I also realized that I had helped pave the way for others to make that journey.

A LANDMARK CEREMONY AT UGA, 1962

On August 16, 1962, I returned to UGA for the summer commencement. It was a hot and sultry but beautiful August day: a cerulean blue sky with fluffy white clouds hovering overhead, a perfectly glorious day for a commencement.

A convoy of cars that transported approximately seventy-four family members, friends, and church members wended its way down Highway 78 to Athens. I didn't seek permission to invite others this time; I just invited them to attend the momentous event.

The group included my mother, brother, sister-in-law, nephew, and my aunt, Emma Joe Ward. Also in attendance were my minister, Rev. Lovett; former high school band director, B. Wayne Walton; my friend and mentor, Jesse Hill Jr.; Margaret Davis Bowens; and many other proud well-wishers. I was happy to have friends, college classmates, and several church members there to share this special day with me. I felt that the degree accomplishment belonged to all of them because I would never have made it to this point without their love and support.

Though my receiving a master's degree would change UGA forever, there were no news media in attendance to chronicle the event. Why? I don't know. On that day, I didn't care. I was so excited that this day had come, and that history would soon be made in Georgia.

This day would also represent the first time that UGA's commencement had included a large number of African Americans as audience members.

After donning my cap and gown, I proceeded to the line of graduate students and found my place among the graduate music students. No one spoke to me—no students, no faculty members, and no administrators. The veil of silence that had marked most of my time at UGA was still very evident. I wondered at the lack of congeniality that usually typified Southerners. Can you imagine one Black graduate amid 600-plus white graduating students? Except for my guests, I was truly invisible to most of the attendees.

As I stood among the other graduate students, the lone African American, to have my degree conferred, I was overcome with emotion. It felt surreal. This was truly a watershed moment. After over 175 years of an all-white University of Georgia, the institution was about to confer a degree upon an African American. I surmised that things would never be the same at UGA after that day. Other Black students (Charlayne and Hamilton first) would follow and more Blacks would receive degrees. I pondered: "How did I get here to this moment?"

Emerging from my reverie, I noticed that there was a man in front of the processional who wore an official uniform and who was holding a long sword. I wondered if they were expecting trouble, and if he represented the first line of defense. I later learned that the man was the Athens sheriff and that this was a tradition dating back to when there were conflicts and confrontations between the university and Native Americans—not exactly the kind of threat I was expecting.

As the line of march processed into the Fine Arts auditorium to the strains of "Pomp and Circumstance," I saw President O. C. Aderhold, with a heavy medallion gracing the front of his robe, leading the other administrators and faculty members up to the stage. After we were all seated, the commencement program began.

Dr. Irvine S. Ingram, emeritus president of West Georgia College, gave the commencement address. In all honesty, I don't remember much of what he said, but that's not unusual. Graduating students are so excited about receiving their degrees that they are not attuned to the speakers.

Following the commencement address, the awarding of degrees began. This was a summer commencement that included both undergraduate and graduate students. The graduate students received their degrees first. I was one of five students receiving the master's degree in music education. When graduate students were instructed to stand and toss their tassels from the right to the left, a big smile lit up my face. Inwardly, I said: "Yes! This is worth the struggle!" Here I was, a native of Georgia, getting a degree from its flagship public institution of higher learning, and I was part of it on my own terms, with the academic accomplishments to support my heartfelt excitement. When I observe students at current commencements I understand their expressions of joy as they receive their degrees. I felt the very same way on August 16, 1962.

When the ceremony was over, I was unable to have an official photo taken in my cap and gown. We had been instructed to turn in our regalia as we exited the auditorium. We were permitted only to keep our tassels.

My family and friends milled around me outside the Fine Arts building after the ceremony and congratulations abounded. I still have a few

Polaroid photos that were taken by one of my guests. The white graduates and their guests gathered at the top of the hill away from us. Some
of the whites looked at us with curious stares.

I had received an invitation from President Aderhold to attend a reception that was scheduled later that evening, but I opted to return to
Atlanta with my family and friends. I didn't want to spoil this memorable day with more hurtful slights and ostracism; I wanted it to remain
the positive, life-affirming accomplishment that it was.

On our arrival back in Atlanta, we had a celebratory dinner at Paschal's restaurant. It was hosted by my high school band director. After
a sumptuous dinner, I thanked my family and friends for their love and
support while I was at UGA. My journey to UGA had ended, at least for
that degree, and I had succeeded in attaining more than a degree. I had
succeeded in making history.

I received many congratulatory cards and even some gifts after the
commencement. Two days after my graduation, the Black *Atlanta Inquirer* published an article: "First Negro Finishes University of Georgia—
Graduates with Honors." The article was accompanied by a photo of me,
standing under the UGA arch. Conversely, my graduation was not noted
by the *Atlanta Journal/Constitution* newspaper until more than a month
after the event. An article was published on September 26 in the evening
newspaper's back section. It was written by Fred Powledge. In the article, he wrote: "MISS EARLY attended the university's commencement
exercise on Aug. 16th and last Friday, she received her diploma." This
timeline seems problematic since August 16 and "last Friday" are quite a
distance from the actual publication date of September 26. This suggests
that the article was actually printed well after the writing of the article. I
guess the first degree awarded to an African American by UGA was not
considered news.

There was another, even more momentous recognition, however: a
personal letter from Dr. Martin Luther King Jr. that I received shortly
after the commencement and which remains one of my prized possessions. In it he noted, "You have done a superb job, and brought the
state of Georgia closer to the American dream," a commendation that

CHILDHOOD AND FAMILY LIFE

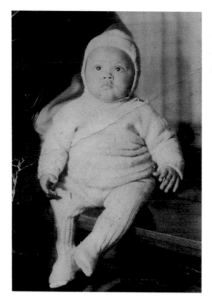

Here I am
at six months
old, 1936.

Ten years old
in Girl Reserves
beanie cap, 1947

With my mother, Annie Ruth Early,
and brother, John, at our Summerhill
home in Atlanta, late 1930s

Celebratory gathering at my father's
restaurant, the Tuxedo Coffee Shop,
in Atlanta, Georgia

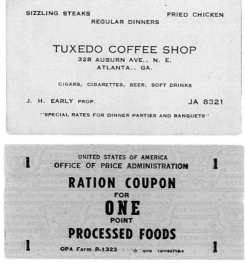

Wartime coupons

My father, John H. Early, was always hard-working and devoted to our family.

My maternal grandmother, Mary Locklin, was an important source of inspiration and strength.

Outside of Turner High School, Atlanta. Proud to be part
of the school's first graduating class, valedictorian, 1953.

My brother John
as an adult

Clark College band with
me in the front center, 1956

Top three graduates at Clark College, 1957. Proud
to be class valedictorian. I am pictured here with
Fred Morgan, salutatorian, and Maxine Moore.

THE UNIVERSITY OF GEORGIA
OFFICE OF THE DIRECTOR OF ADMISSIONS
ATHENS, GEORGIA

To Miss Mary Frances Early
    732 Kennedy Street, N. W.
    Atlanta 18, Georgia

April 25, 1961

THIS IS YOUR OFFICIAL ACCEPTANCE.   PLEASE READ CAREFULLY.

You have been accepted as a student at the University of Georgia. It will be a pleasure to welcome you to the campus and wish you pleasant, profitable days here.

All new students should report to their assigned living quarters at the beginning of Orientation Week for Fall Quarter. (Those entering at Winter or Spring Quarters should report to the Registrar's Office.)

For your convenience and use, an application for housing is enclosed. The University can accept no responsibility for housing unless you are notified in writing that accommodations are reserved for you. Women students must live in dormitories unless married, graduate students, over 23 years of age, or living with parents or relatives. *Freshman men* must live in Reed Hall unless they are veterans, married, or living with parents or relatives.

Please report on time. Late registration fee is $5 for the first day, and thereafter $2 per day through the fourth day, which is the last date, except by special permission, to register for a particular quarter.

If you are a transfer student, a copy of your evaluation of credits is enclosed. Any discrepancy in this copy should be reported to our office within ten days.

Admission has been granted to you in the College of _____ Graduate _____ .

You are classified as _____ Master of Music Education

Please report to the University on _____ June 12, 1961 _____ .

Your admission becomes final when you have fulfilled the conditions checked (X) below. You will not receive further notice from us unless there is some discrepancy in your records.

a. _____ Graduation from high school — Request your high school principal to send us final transcript.
b. _____ Take College Entrance Examination Board Tests and have results filed with this office.

c. _____ Complete your certificate of residence and return to this office.

d. _____ Request your college registrar to send us a supplemental transcript. This transcript must show satisfactory grades and honorable dismissal for your admission to be valid.
e. _____

WALTER N. DANNER
Registrar and Director of Admissions

University of Georgia acceptance letter. After five months of delay tactics by the university, I was finally accepted. Letter dated April 25; received May 12, 1961.

Personal diary entry printed in the *Atlanta Inquirer* and notes describing incidents that followed publication, June 1961.

This article really got me in dutch! I had sent excerpts from my diary to Mr. Holman in lieu of a letter. He printed it, Reverberations! I had my car tires slashed and "Nigger Nigger" written in red paint. Dr. Popovich received threatening letters —supposedly for "acting so gentlemanly to a nigger". I received curious stares from my professors whom I had described. Someone threw a smoke bomb into my room and flew up the stairs in the dorm. Since I wasn't allowed upstairs (for my own safety") so, said the dorm mother — I didn't pursue the *** I just vowed to keep my diary to myself.

Image of my Center Myers dorm room at UGA. Note the two radio clocks by my bed. I was so concerned I would oversleep that I set two alarms, June 1961.

The University of Georgia

hereby confers upon

Mary Frances Early

the degree of

Master of Music Education

together with all the rights, privileges and honors appertaining thereto in consideration of the satisfactory completion of the course prescribed by the Faculty of this University.

In Testimony Whereof, we have hereunto affixed the seal of the University and the signatures of the officers thereof.

Given at Athens, Georgia, on this 16th day of August, 1962.

Chancellor of the University System

Registrar and Secretary of the Faculty

Omer Clyde Aderhold
President of the University

Gerald B. Huff
Dean

UGA diploma and student ID. These official details of my existence at UGA helped me prove to myself I had made great strides for all African Americans wanting a higher education.

This is one of my favorite photos. It
shows me with friends and family who
supported me with their presence at
my graduation, August 1962.

My first band that I organized at John Hope
Elementary School, where I was a music
specialist. These children were ready to show
the world their talents and love of music, 1959.

My love of teaching was founded in a love of music. Here I am at the piano in the early 1960s.

I am pictured, in my Coan Middle School office, with my supervisor, Sara Strong, and my colleague Charlotte Linsey, circa 1970.

The world beckoned, and I took off to
parts unknown. Travel has always been
a huge inspiration to me. Here I am on a
camel in Tunisia, June 2009.

My travel group—Joanne Lincoln, Eugene Bales,
Boon Boonypat, and I—traveled to every continent
but Antarctica. We are pictured here in Athens,
Greece, October 2010.

Church and my faith have been my "Ebenezer" in life. In retirement I was able to be more active, engaging in activities such as mission work. This mission trip was to Slidell, Louisiana, in 2008.

Once I was able to reunite with UGA, I enjoyed Homecoming games with my friends, inviting them to join me in the UGA President's Sky Suites. Here I am with Dorothy Blake, Alfred D. Wyatt, and Joanne Lincoln, 2011.

My "discovery" as UGA's first African American graduate was made possible by Dr. Maurice Daniels, Dean Emeritus of UGA's School of Social Work. (Photo by Nancy Evelyn, 2009)

What an honor to have a lecture series at UGA named after me! I have the amazing graduate students of GAPS (and many others) to thank for this honor. A selection of lecturers over the years includes:

Michael Thurmond, 2015 (Photo by Nancy Evelyn)

Congressman John Lewis, 2011 (Photo by Nancy Evelyn)

Johnetta Cole (right) and Dr. Suzanne Barbour, former dean of the
UGA graduate school, 2016 (Photo by Nancy Evelyn)

Hank Klibanoff, winner of the Pulitzer Prize and a Peabody Award, 2013
(Photo by Nancy Evelyn)

Honorary doctorate from UGA, 2013. Dr. Michael Adams, now president emeritus of the University of Georgia, presents me with this honor. I am the seventy-ninth recipient of an honorary doctorate from UGA.

UGA President's Medal, one of the highest honors the University of Georgia conveys. With UGA president Jere Morehead, 2018.

Who could have imagined in 1962 that a portrait of me would ever hang in the Gordon Jones gallery outside of the president's office? Here I am after the unveiling (2018) with my cousin James Locklin. The portrait was painted by North Carolina artist Richard Wilson.

If you ever want to feel like the world has stopped turning, try getting a phone call from a university president telling you that the University of Georgia has decided to name its outstanding College of Education in your honor. I was speechless when that call came through, and I still have to pinch myself to believe this all really happened. Here I am with President Jere Morehead, Dr. Michelle Cook, UGA vice provost, and Dr. Denise Spangler, dean of the Mary Frances Early College of Education, at the Aderhold Building on UGA's south campus, 2020. (Photo by Peter Frey)

LIFE WORK OF INSPIRING
YOUNG PEOPLE CONTINUES

Here I am with young students at Judia Jackson Harris
Elementary School in Athens, Georgia, 2011. Being with
young, aspiring students remains one of my favorite ways
to give back to our society. (Photo by Nancy Evelyn)

Speaking engagements have been a major part of the recent decades of my life. I never expected to be lecturing to so many people in so many varied venues, but I am honored that people want to hear my story. (Photo by Nancy Evelyn, 2013)

made me feel part of a momentous, historic effort that went far beyond my own experience. I had continued to visit Ebenezer Baptist church throughout my time at UGA. Dr. King's personal letter to me made me feel that I *had* indeed contributed to our fight for civil rights and human dignity—and that was my primary goal.

After the commencement, and before I returned to my job, I responded to some requests for speaking engagements—even one in Chicago. These speaking engagements usually revolved around my experiences at UGA. People had heard or read about my receiving the first degree and were curious about what life on UGA's campus was like. Following these events, life returned to normal and I was able to just relax at home and to reflect on the past year and a half. I had come a long way and I hoped the state of Georgia had too.

CHAPTER SIX

Stepping Up the Professional Ladder in Music Education

I returned to my teaching position at John Hope Elementary in early September 1962. I was so happy to see Mr. Long, fellow teachers, and my students again. Several of the students had written to me during my study leave. I still have those wonderful reminders of why I chose teaching as my career. Some of my students went on to choose music as their career or as an avocation. When I hear from them now by telephone, cards or letters, email or on Facebook, they credit me with inspiring them to engage in music as a lifelong interest.

After I returned to my teaching position, I received a brochure from the Georgia Music Educators Association (GMEA). It was announcing a December GMEA professional music conference that was to be held in Athens. I was already a member of the National Association for Music Educators and its state associate, GMEA. Our dues were paid to the national body with a portion returned to the state organization. I was, therefore, an official member of GMEA.

I was excited about the prospect of attending the state conference for further professional growth. In discussing this with my music resource teacher/supervisor—Mrs. Beatrice Gore—she told me that she, too, wanted to attend the conference in Athens.

And so I contacted Dr. M. J. Newman, GMEA's president, requesting registration forms for Mrs. Gore and me. Dr. Newman had served as my adviser while I was pursuing my degree at UGA. He wrote me back and said that he didn't feel that this would be a good idea because GMEA was not yet integrated. I was astonished! I could go to school with white music teachers at UGA but could not participate in a professional conference with them? What an incongruity! This made no sense to me. I still have a copy of my response letter to Dr. Newman. It expressed my deep disappointment with that decision. Of course, many of the white teachers who would attend the conference had not studied at UGA and Georgia's public schools were still largely segregated. The Atlanta school system had initiated token desegregation in August 1962, but of the 213 students who applied, only 10 were accepted.

I understand the GMEA conference discrimination better now than I did in 1962 but I lost some respect for my former adviser because of this incident. Clearly, GMEA was accepting membership dues from its Black music educators but denying them access to its professional activities.

As a vindication of this incident I would later be elected as GMEA's first Black president and served in that capacity from 1981 to 1983. There would be some pushback against my serving as president, but in the long run the association benefited from my presence, especially in encouraging other Black teachers to join.

Like all state music associations, GMEA also offered other opportunities for its white teachers and students: district music festivals, solo and ensemble festivals, All-State competitions and performances (during state conferences), state board meetings, and district meetings where decisions affecting *all* members were made. Black teachers and students were not allowed to participate in these professional events until the 1970s.

In contrast to the state situation, I found that I *could* attend national music conferences, and I went to Seattle in 1968 for the first of many national meetings. The irony of this situation was not lost on me. GMEA was finally integrated in 1971. When it happened, I threw myself into full participation. By that time, I was teaching at Coan Middle School in northeast Atlanta and entering my advanced band and chorus into all applicable GMEA festivals and competitions.

My real involvement with GMEA began when Dr. Kimball Harriman, then president of GMEA and orchestra director at UGA, appointed me to the GMEA Board of Directors as a member-at-large. Two years later, I was elected as Fifth District (Atlanta and Fulton County schools) chair or president, and thus continued my service on the board. I also served in other elected positions: first vice president, second vice president, president-elect, and finally, as president. When my leadership abilities were recognized, I was called to duty, regardless of the fact that it had been fifteen years since the last female had been elected as president of GMEA.

GMEA is the largest professional organization for music educators in Georgia. Like all other state music educators' associations, it operates under the leadership of our national association (National Association for Music Educators, NAfME). The state of Georgia is divided into twelve districts. I was part of the Fifth District (the schools in the Atlanta and Fulton County school systems). At the time that I was elected GMEA president, our district had a larger number of music educators (elementary through college/university). I think that I won the election with the majority of Fifth District teachers/professors, along with others from across Georgia. At the district level, the chair or president is chosen through a statewide election. All other positions are led by volunteer music educators. The Executive Board of GMEA does not include any volunteer or drafted members. The board is comprised of thirty to forty members. Five or six positions are through appointment; the remainder are through statewide elections.

Although disappointed over the discrimination at GMEA conferences, I happily continued my teaching at John Hope Elementary. The work with general music classes for the entire school, K–7, was enjoyable, but exhausting. Classroom teachers often give their students seat work so that they can catch a breath. Few people realize that music specialists at the elementary level have no such breaks. Classes are scheduled back-to-back and music teachers have few breaks. Lunch often represents the only break from the continual schedule of classes. I scheduled my chorus and band classes on alternate days near the end of the school day. Though already tired, I relished the opportunity to expand the students' musical knowledge in learning to perform the music. The students responded positively to the ever-increasing difficulty of the music that they learned. Both groups excelled to the point that we received invitations to perform outside of school events.

One such event was with Clark College, my alma mater, which hosted a week-long music and arts festival each year. The John Hope Elementary Band had been invited to present a concert in April 1960. Remembering the fact that Dr. Killingsworth had advised against my teaching band, I was very pleased. In April 1963, the John Hope Elementary Chorus was invited to present a similar concert. The students were excited about the prospect of performing for this prestigious event and both groups did an excellent job. Many of my students had never visited a college campus before those concerts. I hoped that one day my young students would aspire to attend college themselves. They understood that they would have to maintain good grades in order to do so and that they would have to take their studies seriously.

As I progressed through my career in music education, I learned that many of my former students indeed went on to attend colleges and universities. Some even attended UGA. Those words of encouragement must have resonated in my young students' minds. Two communications that stand out and make me especially proud are from Bessie Lacey and Veronica West. From Ms. West: "I still remember our days at Coan and Wesley . . . playing my trumpet and singing in the choir. All the wonderful opportunities [Mary Frances Early] afforded [her] students—above and beyond—like taking us to the symphony, to the movies to see *The Sound of Music,* and the special Christmas and Black History programs; all of these had an enormous impact on my life." From Bessie Lacey: "Ms. Mary Frances Early was my most inspirational teacher. Her instruction and advice served me not only in music, but in life. She encouraged me to believe in myself and know that with hard work I could do whatever I pursued. I learned invaluable tools from her that helped me navigate and go beyond the limitations many would say existed. I count [her] as one of God's blessings in my journey."

BACK TO UGA: A SECOND GRADUATE DEGREE

My second sojourn at UGA was very similar to the first—but the overall campus atmosphere was not nearly as hostile.

I returned to UGA in the summer of 1964 to work toward a specialist in music education degree, the EDS. Charlayne and Hamilton had graduated in May 1963. Once again, the news media—local and national—covered their triumphant victory in receiving degrees. I was happy for them because I knew firsthand the price that they had to pay during their tenure at UGA. The ever-present loneliness, the continuing ostracism by many students, the ugly racial taunts, the vandalism to cars, the difficulties that we faced in receiving equal treatment by administrators and some faculty—each of us had to contend with these throughout our matriculation. The three of us remained under the mantle of the 1961 "Student Proclamation." Charlayne, however, did manage to form a close relationship with some of the students, primarily in the School of Journalism. Hamilton, however, remained pretty much a loner in terms of campus relationships.

I was not able to attend their commencement ceremony but sent a congratulatory gift and card to Charlayne. She had left for New York to work on the staff of the *New Yorker* magazine. She sent a thank-you note and asked that I not share her New York address. I surmised that she was weary of so much media attention. And of course, I did not share her address. I still have that note and the one that she sent to me upon my graduation.

In September 1962, just after my commencement, UGA had accepted four freshmen students, the first Black freshmen to enter the institution. Three of them—Alice Henderson, Kerry Rushin, and Harold Black— were from metro Atlanta high schools. Mary Blackwell, the fourth student, was from the Athens school system. Finally, UGA had to open its dormitories beyond the Center Myers first-floor room. Kerry Rushin and Alice Henderson were initially housed in the "Black suite" with Charlayne. Mary Blackwell, from Athens, resided at home.

Harold Black was the first Black male to be housed on UGA's campus. He experienced many unpleasant racial incidents, particularly at his dorm. He was also asked not to return to the First Presbyterian Church when he attended Sunday services with some white students from the Presbyterian Student Center. The minister and his congregation proved that Sunday *is* the most segregated day of the week.

It was obvious that after Charlayne's, Hamilton's, and my time on campus some students and local white citizens were still strongly opposed to the presence of Black students. Alice Henderson left UGA, possibly because of the constant stress and harassment. Kerry Rushin, Harold Black, and Tyrone Barnett (a transfer student) did complete their studies and received their degrees in 1966. Mary Blackwell graduated the next year.

This time around I was housed in Creswell dormitory, rather than the Center Myers freshman dorm. In addition to sharing a communal bathroom, there was a bank of telephones in the hallway of my floor.

I thought it interesting that Mary Ethel Creswell, after whom the dorm was named, was the first woman to receive an undergraduate degree at UGA. In 1913, she was named director of the newly established Home Economics program. She was allowed to take classes and eventually earned a degree. In a way, this fact also supported me to continue on in my studies; I felt part of the bigger picture of changes that individuals wrought on the UGA campus, even though I had little in common with Mary Ethel Creswell.

In addition to the dorm change, I was befriended by a few white graduate students, but not to the extent of having meals together or going to any events.

I remember having a class, Choral Music Materials, with Betty Williford, who would remain a close friend and an Atlanta Public Schools colleague over the years. I also remember studying with Ann Thurmond with whom I took a Modern Music class. (We reconnected in 2007 when she visited Atlanta. We were invited to a lunch at the Watershed restaurant in Decatur, thanks to Lauren Seligman, development director for the College of Education. Ann had written me a letter after seeing me profiled in the Graduate School magazine. In her letter, she stated that she was unaware that I had experienced any problems at UGA. I guess that it's difficult to understand what one does not experience.)

The Modern Music course was designed to teach us important musical compositions from the then contemporary repertoire. These compositions would not be considered "modern" today; they included Stravinsky's *Rite of Spring*, Schoenberg's *Pierrot Lunaire*, Alban Berg's *Six Bagatelles for Strings*, and other selections that are still performed. Some of these compositions are difficult for audiences to understand, but they are firmly ensconced in the orchestra's current canon today.

Dr. John Anderson, the course professor, covered most of the large forms in various genres: symphonies, concerti, operas, sonatas, and string quartets. We listened to the music in class and read about the composers. Our daily assignment was to listen to the assigned compositions on our own. We were expected to be able to recognize and identify any portion of them on listening tests. In those days, there were no CDs or DVDs and certainly no Internet. We used 33 1/3 long-play vinyl recordings. Class members could check out the recordings and listen to them in the Listening Lab.

I so enjoyed the evening sessions when Ann and I would listen and then quiz each other on the various assigned selections. Listening to the music transported me to another world—far away from the tiresome incidents on campus. I could lose myself in the music, all the while learning the themes, variations of themes, form, and other changes. It was in that class that I learned to love the music of Gustav Mahler; I still love his symphonies today. I remember my first reaction to Bela Bartok's Concerto for Orchestra in class. At first listening, I thought that the composition was just a jumble of notes. After a detailed analysis by Dr. Anderson, I recognized the genius of Bartok as he crafted this well-known concerto. It was written in five movements with distinctive Hungarian folk melodies, irregular rhythms, tonality marked by the use of modal harmonies, and delightful dissonances. I particularly enjoyed the second and fourth movements. The second, entitled "Presentation of Pairs," highlights different pairs of instruments (bassoons and oboes, clarinets and flutes—all paired in different intervals). My favorite movement, however, was the fourth, or "Intermezzo." This movement was intoxicating with its flowing melody that is interrupted by changing meters and glissandos by trombones and clarinets. Oh, how I enjoyed unlocking the mysteries of this composition for my students when I taught Music History and Music Appreciation many years later! Other intriguing compositions that I enjoyed in Modern Music included Charles Ives's "The Unanswered Question" and his "Variations on 'America.'" The first was composed in 1908 and revised some years later. This second version represents the one usually performed by orchestras today. The selection begins with peaceful "night" music played by the strings. A lone trumpet poses the unanswered question—"What is the meaning of life or existence?" The winds try to answer the question but are unsuccessful. The question is asked by the trumpet six additional times and each time the winds answer in more strident tones. Their answer is always unsatisfactory. The six-minute composition ends with a final question played by the solo trumpet. In 1964, like today, the tenor of the times makes this important question ever more important. We still have no satisfactory answer.

Ives's "Variations on 'America,'" the popular "My Country 'Tis of Thee," projects a series of rather comical versions of the song. It includes the playing of the piece in simultaneous different keys. Ives remains one of the most inventive American composers.

We also had to research and write reports on the contemporary composers. It was a very comprehensive course. This class helped me tremendously during my teaching career, particularly years later when I taught Music History and Music Appreciation at Clark Atlanta University. Once again, my grades were excellent; the classes were demanding but my heart was in it.

I had a new adviser for the specialist degree: Dr. James E. Dooley. He was very helpful in building my schedule of courses for the degree. He told me that I could request the transfer of additional course credits from my work at the University of Michigan. I did this, and, receiving nine hours, I was able to skip going to the UGA campus during the summer of 1965.

I matriculated during the summers of 1964, 1966, and 1967, receiving the specialist's certificate in 1967. UGA changed the certificate to a degree in 1971. While I was proud of my certificate, I wanted to get the actual degree. Dr. Louis Castenell, then dean of the College of Education, was kind enough to make that happen some years later. I still appreciate his efforts on my behalf. I now have both degrees in my possession.

Many people asked me why I returned to UGA after the master's degree. My reply was simple: There were still too few African American students on campus. Others asked if the campus and surrounding areas were still dangerous. I respond to that question with the story of Lemuel Penn.

In July 1964, an African American Army officer, Lemuel Penn, was murdered in Madison County, Georgia, on the Broad River bridge that crosses into Elbert County, not far from Colbert, Georgia, just outside of Athens. He and two companions (Charles E. Brown and John D. Howard) were driving from Fort Benning, after serving in reserve training, back to Washington, D.C. Penn was an assistant superintendent for the Washington, D.C. school system. He was dressed in military uniform and driving an attractive automobile. He and his companions stopped at a service station in Athens and were observed by some Ku Klux Klansmen. Still smoldering from the passage of the Civil Rights Act earlier that month, the Klansmen followed the car out of town and shot Penn in the head through the windows of his car. While the men who perpetrated the crime were charged with first-degree murder, the all-white jury acquitted them. It was only later that they were tried and convicted on conspiracy charges and sent to federal prison with ten-year sentences. So, yes, the potential for danger was still present during the mid-sixties when I returned to UGA for a second degree.

Another student, Darlyne Killian, was enrolled at UGA in 1964. Though from Atlanta, Darlyne was housed in the married students' apartments with her husband, Herty Killian. Herty was part of the Killian family at whose home Hamilton Holmes had lived while at UGA. Darlyne was pursuing a master's degree in art education. In 1966, she moved to Creswell Hall. Darlyne, a free-spirited African American art teacher in the Atlanta Public Schools, and I became fast friends. Though she had a roommate at UGA, we ate meals together and enjoyed many adventures. One such experience occurred when we decided to test the Athens city desegregation policies. We went to the Howard Johnson restaurant that was located on Broad Street for lunch. We entered the restaurant, sat in a booth, and waited for a waitress to take our orders. No one ordered us to leave, but after approximately twenty minutes, we determined that no one wanted to serve us. Darlyne was taking a course in statistics and was experiencing problems in understanding the terminology. I had taken a statistics course and had successfully passed it. We discussed problems with standard deviation, t scores, median/mean, correlation, and other things that puzzled her. An hour passed; then two hours; then three hours, and finally a surly waitress came to take our orders. We felt triumphant as we finished our lunch and left. Neither of us had a class after noon that day—so we were determined to be served or to be asked to leave. We never returned to the Howard Johnson restaurant for lunch. Interestingly, we often dined at a "white" cafeteria on Alps Road and never experienced a problem. These excursions occurred on Sundays because Snelling Hall did not provide meals on that day.

Another experience that amused us was the day that we decided to travel to Atlanta for a Braves baseball game. The Braves team came to Atlanta in 1966 and we wanted to see a game. Though we were graduate students, we were required to return to the dorm before midnight. Creswell's doors were locked each night at midnight at that time. We had no idea if we could actually get back to Athens and the dorm before 12:00 a.m., but we were determined that we would attend the game. The game was exciting; our team won; and we started the trip back to Athens with the hope that we would not get locked out. Though Darlyne probably exceeded the speed limit while driving, we arrived at the dorm ten minutes after midnight. Needless to say, we were not cheerfully welcomed as the dorm attendant had to open the door for us!

The remainder of my studies for the Ed.S degree at UGA progressed smoothly, partly because I now had someone with whom to share time in dining and events. After I left in 1967, Darlyne received her master's degree in art education and continued on to earn the specialist degree.

My adviser, Dr. Dooley, was pleased with my academic progress and encouraged me to return to UGA for the doctorate in music education. He also offered an assistantship that would provide some remuneration for my work. He reminded me that the specialist degree, with its requisite forty-five hours beyond the master's, represented the stepping-stone to the doctorate—and that most of those hours would count toward the doctorate. I was aware of this, but told him that I could not afford to abandon my job and my home responsibilities at the time. I promised to keep this offer in mind for the future.

In 1968, I received an invitation from the UGA Music Department to be inducted into Pi Kappa Lambda, a national music honor society. This invitation was based upon my aggregate GPA of 4.04; I accepted the honor but did not attend the induction ceremony because of a previously scheduled school concert. I did, however, receive my pin and certificate of membership. I still have and treasure those items today.

After the Pi Kappa Lambda induction in 1968, I heard nothing from UGA. It was as though I had never attended. One would think that the Alumni Association would have contacted me for membership, but that did not happen. I was summarily forgotten as the first person of my race to receive a degree. And so I placed UGA at the back of my mind and went on with my career. I was, initially, angry and hurt over the slight but my inner strength helped me to overcome that hurt and anger, and my career, which was very demanding, was deeply satisfying.

As the years rolled by, I recognized the fact that those who chose to ignore my contribution to UGA's desegregation history were no longer relevant.

CHAPTER SEVEN

Beyond UGA:
My Professional Career Broadens

———

Affter a few additional years at John Hope Elementary School, I followed Mr. Long to Wesley Avenue Elementary, a larger school with over a thousand students. I worked very hard teaching ten general music classes a day and developing an outstanding band, chorus, and recorder ensemble. Many elementary music specialists use the song flute as a vehicle for teaching music notation. I had observed the use of recorders both at UGA and at music conferences and decided that I wanted to form a recorder consort at Wesley. I discussed this idea with Polly Moore, who was my music supervisor. She agreed that the recorder was a much better instrument than the song flute. She warned me that authentic or wood recorders were expensive. I then discussed the idea with Mr. Long. He told me that I could spend up to $500 to purchase recorders.

Polly Moore took me to George Kelischek's music studio. He demonstrated the soprano, alto, and tenor recorders from his inventory. I purchased ten soprano, four alto, and two tenor recorders. I decided to try their use first with a select after-school group. After purchasing suitable recorder method books, I began a twice weekly recorder class. The students progressed rapidly. They enjoyed playing simple folk melodies like "Frère Jacques" and then, progressively, Renaissance melodies that were harmonized. These were indeed busy but fulfilling days for me. In my second year of teaching at Wesley, I received Teacher of the Year recognition as I had done at John Hope.

In 1968, Mr. Long informed me that he was being transferred to the newly built Coan Middle School, the first middle school to be established in Georgia. He asked me to accompany him on this new venture, and I readily agreed. I truly valued his superb support of the music program and knew that together we could develop and forge a high-quality middle school music program. And that we did!

The only problem was that I was, initially, the only music teacher. I taught band, chorus, and general music to a large number of students. The band area was located on one end of the ground floor; the chorus room was on the opposite end. When we had programs, I would have to race from one end of the hall to warm up the chorus and then run to the other end to warm up the band.

Eventually, at my request, Mr. Long hired a chorus teacher and a general music teacher to assist me with this very large music program. Veronica Scott, who had student taught under my supervision, served as the choral teacher, and Dianne Mayfield served as a general music teacher. The following school year, John Johnson was hired to assist me with band classes. He taught two beginner band classes and a general music class. He also taught two social studies classes. I taught advanced band, intermediate band, a general music class, and humanities. Mrs. Scott taught three choral classes and two general music courses. Ms. Mayfield taught three general music classes. We had a very comprehensive music program and our students excelled both musically and academically.

Since GMEA had not yet racially integrated its membership, I decided to take the band to an all-Black band festival that was held in Fort Valley, Georgia. I had worked very hard with the advanced band and wanted to see how the band was progressing in their musicianship. The festival used three male adjudicators to evaluate each band. After we performed a march and two concert selections, I felt that my students had performed well. When I received the adjudication forms from the judges, I found that we had earned a 1, or Superior, rating. One of the judges however, had commented that the band played quite well for a female conductor. I didn't like this female discrimination, so I approached the judge and asked what he meant by this comment. He told me that it was rare for bands to have a lady conductor. I told him that female band teachers study the same curriculum as male band teachers. In retrospect,

I realize that I should not have approached the judge after receiving his comments. I was miffed, however, with this chauvinism.

After that year, GMEA was integrated and we took our performing groups to the GMEA Fifth District music festivals. They always received ratings of Excellent or Superior. The first year when GMEA was integrated, I prepared the band for the competition. The three adjudicators each rated the band's performance as 2 or Excellent. (Adjudication ratings ranged from 1 to 5.) After reading the judges' comments to my band students, we decided that we would improve our performance for the following year. I purchased Charles Bradley's high-quality mouthpieces for each clarinet and saxophone player. I did this because one of the judges had commented that we had intonation problems in the reed section. I selected level 3 selections for the band and set up daily after-school sectional rehearsals for each week. The students worked hard to correct notes, dynamic changes, difficult rhythmic passages, and blend. I had chosen a march for the first selection, the five-movement European Folk Tune Suite for the second selection, and Menuetto, the third movement from Mozart's Symphony No. 40. I observed that even when some students were not involved in sectionals, they went to the practice rooms to work out parts that were difficult. We worked very hard for this second trip to GMEA's music festival.

When the day arrived, the students looked resplendent in their red blazers, white shirts or blouses, and black pants or skirts. A sense of wonderment filled me as I conducted the band in its program. I was so proud of my students. They performed with a maturity beyond their ages. When we received the ratings, we were exuberant with the results. We had indeed earned a Superior rating from each judge. One judge, however, commented that with such a high-caliber band, we needed the addition of double reeds to complete our instrumentation. I had substituted a single saxophone to play an exposed oboe part and the bassoon parts were covered by other instruments. When I shared the judges' comments with Mr. Long, he expressed his pride in our rating and performance. He also authorized the purchase of a first-line oboe and bassoon. He then arranged a cake and ice cream victory event for the band.

When Coan opened as a new school, I was able to purchase a large number of instruments—ones that students don't generally buy. They included a piccolo, an alto clarinet, a bass clarinet, a tenor and baritone saxophone, French horns, baritone horns and tuba, a bass drum, cymbals, and a set of tympani. With the addition of double reeds, our instrumentation was almost complete. With this level of support from a principal, one could only work tirelessly to do one's best.

In addition to our fostering a healthy performing arts program at Coan, I also expanded the general music offerings through the introduction of classroom guitar and humanities.

INTRODUCING GUITAR STUDIES IN ATLANTA

One such offering turned out to be a gift to the process of teaching music in general: a guitar program. The guitar program came about when Mr. Long told me that he wanted me to teach guitar during the summer months. The program was being sponsored by the Atlanta Parks and Recreation Department and our school and participating students would receive free acoustic guitars from the city. I told Mr. Long that I had no experience with guitars and therefore couldn't teach the instrument. He replied that he was confident that I could manage the program and that I would be paid through the Parks and Recreation Department for the summer months. I knew then that he had already accepted the program and that I'd better become acquainted with the guitar and how to teach it.

I purchased an acoustic guitar, found a promising guitar method book, and began learning how to play. It wasn't too difficult except for giving me sore fingers from the steel strings. (We were to use steel-string guitars rather than nylon-string classical guitars.)

The summer began with my teaching two classes of guitar each day. The two classes included twenty students each. It was fun to open the world of guitar to these inner-city students. In addition to the free lunches to nourish their bodies, they were given guitar lessons to nourish their souls. The program was so successful that the *Atlanta Journal* newspaper published a lengthy article about this wonderful summer program for inner-city kids. The students were proud because the reporter also included a photo of some of them playing their guitars.

I was hooked! I used the guitars in my one general music class during the school year and received a more positive response from the students. I found that with an actual guitar in their hands, they were more engaged in understanding and learning the basics of music. They also sang with enthusiasm—something that they didn't do when using the music textbooks. They had to sing so that their chords would be accompanied with the melodies.

Helen Elliott, of Educational Productions, heard about the summer guitar program and met with me to offer the use of an electric guitar station to supplement the acoustic guitars. The only stipulation was that I was asked to develop an audiovisual program based on the *Guitar Magic* method book that she had compiled. She had completed three audiovisual lessons but wanted a music educator to develop the remaining thirty-two lessons. After observing my general music guitar classes, she was confident that I could do this. I was also to write a teacher's manual that outlined objectives and teaching strategies for each lesson. I took this on, writing the lessons on story boards with illustrations for the filmstrips. Working until late night at home, I completed the thirty-two lessons by the end of the school year and proceeded to pilot the program and manual with another group of students that summer. This was very exciting! The students sat at thirty guitar stations that were equipped with an electric guitar, headphones, a music stand, and the *Guitar Magic* method book. The lessons were on filmstrips that were synchronized with song accompaniments played by a professional band. The teacher's station had the capability of giving verbal instructions to the students and monitoring individual students as they progressed through the lessons.

The students practiced on the acoustic guitars at the end of the recorded lesson to refine what they had learned. It was truly *magic*. Eventually, they wanted to learn to play melodies. At that point, they were only learning chordal accompaniments. They envisioned themselves as guitar rock stars like Michael Jackson. I told them that they had to learn to read music notation if they were to play melodies. They responded enthusiastically because they were self-motivated. I researched simple melodies, beginning with three-note melodies such as "Hot Cross Buns" and progressing to five-note melodies, and so forth, that they could perform. They learned music notation and note values.

Though I was paid for my work on the audiovisual *Guitar Magic* lessons and the teacher's manual, I failed to apply for copyright protection. This was to cause problems that I didn't anticipate.

We had many visitors to observe our classes throughout the year as other teachers and administrators wanted to see this innovative program that was motivating young students. Educational Productions even funded a trip to Jacksonville, Florida, for ten of my students and me. The Jacksonville school system was considering the purchase of this expensive program and hardware for its schools. The superintendent and school board wanted to see a live demonstration of the program. Mr. Long sought and received permission for our students to go to Jacksonville.

I chose my best guitar students by audition. The ten students who were chosen had never flown in an airplane before, and many had never left the state of Georgia. They were very excited about the impending trip. We did preparation for the demonstration after school hours for several weeks, flew to Jacksonville, and performed several lessons from the guitar program. Educational Productions had sent ten electronic guitar stations with a teacher monitor. The students demonstrated the use of the acoustic guitars, playing several songs accompanied by their singing. I don't know if Jacksonville purchased the program, but I do know that my students had an experience that they will never forget.

The program was expanded at Coan Middle School because I coached the choral and general music teachers so that they could also use *Guitar Magic* with students. The Atlanta Public Schools' Staff Development requested that I offer an in-service guitar class for system music teachers. Having heard of the success of the program, other music teachers wanted to learn the instrument so that they could include guitar in their curricula. Fifty teachers registered for the after-school course. Participants had to purchase their own guitars and a *Guitar Magic* method book. The class was held after school hours five days a week for two

months. Though tired after a full day of teaching at Coan, the teachers' enthusiasm gave me energy! Initially, I had headaches with the task
of assisting teachers to tune their guitars (not all music teachers have
perfect pitch . . .). Eventually, however, we were able to accomplish this
in a shorter amount of time. I was inspired with how well the teachers
embraced the various guitar techniques. And of course, they sang in
beautiful harmony. At the end of the in-service course we presented a
final concert. The room was crowded with the teachers' principals, other
music teachers, and administrators. It was an exhilarating experience
to hear fifty music teachers sing and play with confidence. Since the
teacher participants had mastered the basics of playing and teaching
guitar, I hoped that their principals would find the resources to purchase
instruments for their students.

Before I left Coan for a promotional position, a salesman from Ken
Stanton's music store came to my office to show me a new guitar program. It had been developed by the world-famous guitarist Chet Atkins
and his brother, Jim. When he demonstrated this program for me, I told
him that it hadn't been developed by Chet Atkins and his brother—it
had been written by me. He, of course, didn't believe me until I pulled
the story boards that I had developed from my file cabinet. He was
dumbfounded and left shaking his head.

I contacted Helen Elliott and asked why the Atkinses had the program. She told me that others in her family who co-owned Educational
Productions had sold the program to Chet Atkins. She pointed out the
fact that I had been paid for my efforts in writing it and that the program
had not been copyrighted. She said that the teacher's manual had not
been sold to the Atkins brothers.

When I contacted my attorney, he told me that my error in not ob-
taining a copyright would not bode well for me. He also said that Chet
Atkins was vice president of RCA Records and that their lawyers would
"eat me alive" if I chose the path of litigation.

I learned a valuable lesson: always have your work copyrighted
if you want to receive credit for it! Of course, the Atkinses renamed
the program (F.A.M.E.) and added a few new songs at the back of the
Guitar Magic method book. The audiovisual lessons weren't changed

that much from what Helen and I had written. I guess that I should have felt flattered that they thought the program was worthy of carrying their name, but I knew that they didn't write most of it. This program represented my very first published work, and I felt that I had been robbed of my creative efforts. I discussed this situation with my mother. She told me that I should accept the incident as a life lesson learned. She reminded me that we grow from disappointments and failures in life because we learn from them. I appreciated this wisdom from my mother. I knew that she was right. I was thirty-four years of age and still considered my mother as my role model—we were not only daughter and mother but also best friends. I could discuss anything with her and expect to get sage advice. I treasured that bond between us because she was always supportive of my professional career but never hesitant about sharing her insights.

It sometimes seems that when life is moving along smoothly, bad things are bound to happen. For me it happened when, tragically, my mother died in July 1970. She had a brief illness and after a few weeks in the hospital, she died. Her death left a huge void in my life because we had such a special bond. I had continued to live with her after the UGA years. She was an avid baseball fan and we always watched the Atlanta Braves on television. She considered Hank Aaron a superstar and we enjoyed attending baseball games together at the Atlanta stadium so that we could see him in real time. Occasionally Mom would allow me to treat her to dinner at Paschal's or Frazier's restaurant. This happened most often for special days such as her birthday or a holiday, but for the most part she preferred cooking at home. It seemed that her greatest joy was to accompany me to concerts when my students performed. She was always there to see me conduct and to hear the students perform.

After Mother's death, I devoted even more time to strengthening the music program at Coan Middle School. I had added a course in humanities that was co-taught by Darlyne Killian, the art teacher, and me. Darlyne and I had a close friendship because she too was a UGA graduate. We had enjoyed some fun times together when I returned to UGA for my second degree. Now, we were working at the same school and sharing the joy of teaching together. Darlyne's daughter Darnita was a talented member of my advanced band. (After I left UGA, Darlyne completed her master's and a specialist degree in art.) Years later, after we had both retired, I journeyed to Athens and witnessed Darlyne being recognized for her pioneering accomplishment: she was honored by the UGA Art Department for being the first Black person to earn a master's degree in art. I was so very proud of her.

My guitar students performed at Lenox Square as part of the Christmas concerts, performed at school programs, and were presented in a session at the Music Educators' National Conference in Atlanta. I entitled the session "Using the Guitar to Educate, Motivate, and Stimulate." The session was well attended and was enthusiastically received. I don't know if Coan was the first school that used the guitar as a major curriculum component, but the instrument seemed to blossom throughout the system and the state. Several of our colleges and universities now offer guitar as a degree major, Georgia State University and the University of Georgia among them. GMEA now includes guitar as a division along with chorus, band, and orchestra. Guitar ensembles are often included as performing groups at state conferences. I believe that this evolved because the guitar is a personal instrument that is easily portable, is less expensive than traditional band instruments, and is highly satisfying as a vehicle of personal expression.

MY CAREER IN PROFESSIONAL MUSIC CONFERENCES

The Music Educators National Conference held in Atlanta represented the beginning of my involvement in professional music conferences as a presenter.

In 1973, I was promoted from my teaching position to music resource teacher/supervisor for Area 5 in the Atlanta Public Schools. Though I was proud to receive the promotion, I hated to leave the direct teaching of students. After 15 years of teaching, I would no longer have students of my own. I would have to work through other teachers instead.

The new position was a supervisory job. The Atlanta public school system was divided into five areas, with a music supervisor for each area. I enjoyed working with the other four music supervisors and the system's coordinator/director of music, Dr. Robert Wagonner.

I supervised the Area 5 music teachers in elementary, middle, and high schools (choral, instrumental, and general music). Since I had taught in each of these areas, I had no difficulty in assisting teachers to foster strong music programs at their schools. Two years later, the school system reorganized and reduced the number of areas to three. I was moved to Area 2 in the same position.

Though I now had many more schools and teachers to supervise, I was able to make frequent visits to schools where assistance was most needed. I also visited schools that had excellent music teachers.

Music teachers are among the most isolated teachers in a school. Unlike classroom teachers or those in specific middle/high school disciplines, music teachers are usually the only one in their discipline in their school. They therefore have no one with whom to share problems or successes. All music teachers welcome assistance or positive feedback. That was my job.

Observing the fact that some principals did not steer funds to the elementary general music program, I requested area funds to purchase choral octavos, classroom items such as guitars, Orff instruments, and choir chimes or hand bells. These I issued on loan to those teachers who requested them. The purchase of octavo music helped to prevent the practice of copying music and violating the copyright law. We thus had an extensive choral library and a collection of instruments that could be used to enhance general music at the elementary level.

With regard to the addition of hand bells, I attended a national music conference in San Antonio, Texas, and observed the use of choir chimes and hand bells with elementary students. When I returned to Atlanta, I requested the purchase of a set of choir chimes for Area 2.

I was so fortunate throughout most of my career to have supportive administrators who shared my passion for a first-class music education program. Mrs. Joan Zion, the assistant superintendent for Area 2, was truly supportive. My aspirations for the music program matched her vision. She never refused a request that she felt was in the best interest of our students.

I placed the choir chimes with a creative teacher, and the results were phenomenal. After observing Roselyn Lewis's students performing with the choir chimes at a principals' meeting, other principals asked for information on how to purchase a set.

Soon, principals began to purchase the more expensive hand bells. I organized in-service workshops for teachers so that they could learn the proper techniques for teaching these instruments. Many schools boasted choir chime or hand bell ensembles as part of their curriculum. Students learned to read music and to perform at a high level of musicality. This, of course, boosted their self-esteem. One of my fondest memories while I was in a supervisory position was an All-City Music Festival that was held at the Atlanta Civic Center. We not only included all-city bands, choruses, and orchestras—we also included a citywide hand bell and choir chimes ensemble. It was composed of talented students from several schools. This ensemble of a hundred students performed several selections under the direction of Ms. Roselyn Lewis. What a glorious sound!

A by-product of this school-based program was the inclusion of hand bell ensembles in metro churches that had never heard of the instruments. And, of course, the music teachers taught and directed the church ensembles. This was a shining example of the broad community being positively impacted by school curricula.

FULBRIGHT-HAYS TRAVEL FELLOWSHIPS

In 1974, the Atlanta Public Schools and Fulton County Schools were offered the opportunity to participate in a Fulbright-Hays Fellowship initiative. The initiative allowed teachers and supervisory personnel to travel to West Africa for a six-week study of its culture.

Potential candidates were interviewed over the period of a month, and fifteen participants were selected. I was fortunate to be selected for this travel opportunity. It would represent my first trip abroad, and I was extremely excited about this educational opportunity.

We had weekly workshops in preparation for the trip over a period of two months. We also had a dinner at the home of one of the participants, where we dined on authentic West African food. The workshops and dinner led to a connection with my future travel partners: Joanne Lincoln and Eugene Bales. My supervisors approved the trip, but I had to use annual leave for the duration.

We traveled to Senegal, Ghana, and Nigeria. We visited major cities and cultural events. We also had the pleasure of living with an African family for an entire week. Our diverse group absorbed the wonders of an entirely different culture.

We purchased authentic artifacts to take back to the school systems, and I was appointed as coordinator for the purchases. Naturally, we also made personal purchases of artifacts and authentic clothing. I still have a beautiful dress that was created for me in Senegal.

When we returned to Atlanta, we presented the superintendent, Dr. Alonzo Crim, with a gift and highlights of the trip. We also presented African-specific sessions to student groups at various venues. We were tasked with sharing our rich resources with students and teachers. We shared a slide presentation (there was no PowerPoint software at that time). We exhibited the instruments and other artifacts that we had purchased for the school system. The students and teachers responded enthusiastically to our educational sessions. This was my first trip abroad, but certainly not my last.

In 1978, a similar Fulbright-Hays initiative was offered to visit Brazil. This, too, was an exhilarating experience. Participants had to register for preparation classes through Georgia State University. We spent several weeks in studying the Portuguese language and learning what to expect as to the culture of the country. We traveled throughout Brazil from the Amazonas to central Brazil and then to the coast, visiting Rio, Bahia, Brasilia, Belo Horizonte, Recife, and other major cities. Once again, we had the opportunity to live with a family for a week. Language posed a big problem for many of us. We had studied the Portuguese language in our preparatory classes, but the people spoke so rapidly that it was difficult to understand them. We found that Brazil is a beautiful country with many varying landscapes. It was breathtaking to see the Christ the Redeemer statue perched high on Mount Corcovado. The food was equally diverse and delicious.

Once again, we shared our experiences with student groups and their teachers back home in Atlanta. Each of these travel experiences occurred during the summer months, and so our work with students and teachers was basically not interrupted.

MY ASSOCIATION WITH GMEA

On another front and as mentioned earlier, music teachers were encouraged to join our state and national professional organizations (GMEA/ NAfME) and to participate in the district meetings, All-State competitions, and music festivals with their bands, choruses, and orchestras.

This strategy worked to improve the overall musicianship of students as well as to encourage teacher professional leadership positions within the organization. Some teachers (generally the white teachers) had already been active in professional organizations, but many more now gained the confidence to do so. Music festivals and All-State competitions represent evaluation vehicles for music teachers. We observed a marked improvement as teachers sought to prepare their performance groups for top ratings.

GMEA had only been integrated for roughly ten years, and it took some time to bring larger participation to fruition.

I worked with the elementary music teachers to organize an area-wide Elementary Honor Chorus. The students were selected by audition and represented all schools in the area. Rehearsals were held once weekly after school hours.

I had wonderful support from the area superintendent and particularly the assistant area superintendent, Mrs. Joan Zion. The principals, too, embraced this stellar group of elementary singers. The Area 2 Honor Chorus eventually evolved into a systemwide Elementary Honor Chorus. I was asked to conduct the chorus in its debut performance, which was held at the GMEA music conference in Columbus, Georgia. The Honor Chorus received enthusiastic applause from the conference attendees.

As mentioned earlier, after being denied participation in the 1962 GMEA conference, I was elected as president of this statewide music organization in 1980. This was the first time that an African American had been elected as president. I felt a deep sense of responsibility to do a good job and served in this position from 1981 to 1983.

As president, I traveled throughout the state to attend district meetings and planned two state conferences with statewide chairs of the various divisions. When I became state president of GMEA, I received full support from the APS superintendent of schools, Dr. Alonzo Crim, and from my immediate supervisors at the area office.

They allowed me to adjust my work schedule to accommodate the demands of this statewide position. I didn't take advantage of this privilege, but worked full days at the area office and then went to the GMEA office, which was on West Peachtree Street. I would work until late at night handling the correspondence and other tasks that came with the presidency. During the day, the executive secretary, Dr. Don Robinson, handled the association's business. I received permission to use annual leave for the days that I would be out of the office for state or national travel.

My first statewide conference was held at Jekyll Island. After months of careful planning with the divisional chairs (Elementary, Band, Chorus, Orchestra, College, Student division, and Piano) to obtain outstanding clinicians/consultants, select performing groups, and All-State conductors, we were ready for our conference.

The preregistration for attendance was among the largest in GMEA's history. That was partly due to the larger number of African American music teachers registered to attend. They had a Black president and wanted to support that position as well as to grow professionally. I was so humbled and gratified for their support.

The board meeting that preceded the conference sessions also included seven African Americans as members. This was a *first*—because before my presidency, there were, at the most, two Black board members.

As I stood at the podium for the opening night's general session and looked out on the large, very diverse audience, I had tears in my eyes.

I thanked God for bringing me to that place at that time. It was a beautiful sight to see. GMEA, the state affiliate of the National Association for Music Educators, had come a long way since 1962 when I was told that I could not attend the state conference.

The national executive secretary, Dr. Don Dillon, served as the keynote speaker. He praised GMEA for its forward vision and progress in terms of racial inclusiveness.

The elegant President's Reception—planned and implemented by my friend and colleague Dr. Alfred D. Wyatt Sr.—followed the opening session. This represented another first. Previous Presidents' Receptions involved only the Executive Board. I wanted all members to enjoy a celebratory reception. Alfred Wyatt solicited private funds to finance the reception. It provided me the opportunity to meet and greet so many of my music colleagues from all over the state, and to thank them for their attendance. After three days of exceptional sessions and performances by outstanding band, choral, orchestra, and piano groups, we closed the conference with wonderful All-State performances. We began the last day with an all-conference breakfast. I had asked former GMEA president Max Noah (one of GMEA'S first presidents) to deliver the grace, and Polly Moore, my former music resource teacher and former GMEA president (fifteen years earlier) to deliver the keynote address. Dr. T. Marshall Jones, Student Music Educators National Conference (MENC) chair, presented the first ever Student MENC award for conference participation. An outstanding cellist from UGA provided beautiful music. It was a lovely closing event.

After the conference, I received many complimentary calls, letters, and cards from various attendees. I shared these plaudits with the organizing committee in a postconference debriefing session; I knew that the conference's success was the result of team effort. Some of the comments I received heartened me considerably; in many ways, I felt all my work and expertise was vindicated. There were people who thought I might not do a good job, but here was proof that I had: Dr. Don Tabel of Georgia State University said, "First, let me congratulate you on the splendid convention of the GMEA. From my point of view and from that of others with whom I spoke, this was one of the best conventions which GMEA has had." Dr. Olin Parker, a respected UGA music professor, commented: "I wanted to again commend you on the manner and professional standard which you yourself set as an individual when you were presiding at the various sessions. Just a week before our conference, I was at the Missouri Educators Association Annual Conference in Osage Beach, Missouri. Their conference was a good one, but I was mighty pleased with the standards which you led us at our own conference." And Dr. Ronald L. Wahn, another UGA music professor, wrote: "It was one of the best I have ever attended. Some of my colleagues thought it was much better than the national. The final breakfast was just one of the nicest events I have attended. You have done a great job as our leader." Praise like this went a long way in steeling me against prejudice and the assumption that I would not succeed.

As president of Georgia's music affiliate organization, I also participated in the National Assembly, which included the MENC (now NAfME) national officers and each of the state affiliate presidents. I was the only African American president. We met at the National Headquarters in Reston, Virginia. The three-day meeting also included a trip to Capitol Hill where we met with our respective state senators and congressmen. We were charged with the task of advocating for support of music education.

I also served on the SDMENC or Southern Divisional Board of Directors, which is comprised of presidents of the southern state affiliate organizations. Once again, I was the lone Black participant.

My second GMEA conference was held in Columbus, Georgia. Things must have gone too well for the first conference because this conference presented many challenges. The first foreboding sign appeared as I drove to Columbus. I had left for the journey after work, driving alone, and had a flat tire. I was completely out of my element because I had no idea of how to change a tire. I sat on the side of the road as cars, even state patrol cars, sped by.

Finally, an elderly white gentleman stopped to give me aid. He changed the flat tire to my "donut" spare and asked me to follow him to the nearest exit where I could find a service station. He remained with me until a new tire was installed and refused to accept any money for his beyond-the-call of duty help. This selfless demonstration of kindness gave me the resolve to "give forward" whenever I observed someone in need of assistance.

I proceeded to Columbus and checked into the hotel. While listening to the evening news, I discovered that inclement weather was predicted for Atlanta and the surrounding areas; indeed, throughout Georgia. That prediction proved true as the next morning's news reported snow and icy roads throughout the state.

I received a call from our national president, Dr. Russell Getz, who was to serve as keynote speaker. He said that his plane from Pennsylvania had been delayed because of inclement weather in Georgia. I told him that I would prefer that he not come to the conference because we didn't want to put his life at risk.

The Southern Division president, Dr. Robert Surplus, was able to attend because he came a day before the bad weather arrived. When I told Dr. Surplus that our national president would not be able to attend, he readily agreed to serve as keynote speaker.

Calls came throughout the day regarding others, including consultants and presenters who would not be able to attend. I had the problem of who would present the multiplicity of sessions that had been scheduled. Several of the exhibitors coming from varied states also expressed their regrets at not being able to attend. After talking with our executive secretary, Don Robinson, who was already in Columbus to handle registration, I decided that we would reimburse members their meal costs for divisional luncheons if they were unable to get to the conference.

I placed calls to Columbus College to ask the Music Department chairman if he could solicit professors to handle various sessions. I also called other GMEA members who were already there for the board meeting and asked the same.

Somehow, we got through the three days with few cancelled sessions. This was real teamwork. The All-State performances were also held on schedule because each of the guest conductors had come to Columbus early to make final preparations. Many music teachers had also brought their All-State students to Columbus early. The guest conductors reported that they had sufficient numbers of students to proceed with the anticipated performances.

I received some irate calls from school superintendents and principals. They were upset because their All-State students were not able to attend because of the weather. They wanted me to postpone the All-State events and reschedule them for a future date. Parents felt that the honor of participating in All-State was not as important as their children's safety and kept their children at home.

I apologized to the administrators but pointed out that the students who *were* there had the right to go ahead with the prestigious experience. This was a judgment call that I had to make, and I took full responsibility.

When the conference ended, I dreaded the final financial report for the conference. I feared that we would probably experience a large deficit. That, however, was not the case. We didn't have a deficit, though we had refunded the meal costs to those who could not attend. With good teamwork and the can-do attitude of many people, my second GMEA conference had been successful despite the bad weather.

At the end of the year, I passed the gavel to the new president and breathed a sigh of relief. The 1981–1983 term had been effective. I continued to work with GMEA on the Board of Directors as second vice president, past presidents' representative, and on the editorial committee of the *Georgia Music News*. In 1992, I received GMEA's Distinguished Service award. This award represents the organization's highest recognition given to a music educator. I believe that my experiences and struggles at UGA helped me to be successful in this and many other pioneering efforts.

DIRECTOR OF MUSIC FOR ATLANTA'S PUBLIC SCHOOLS

In the year following my GMEA presidency, I was promoted to the position of director of music for the Atlanta Public Schools. This was the highest position in the APS for any discipline and truly the pinnacle of my career.

I was responsible for the overall music curriculum, the entire music budget, purchase of music textbooks, band uniforms, pianos, and musical instruments, as well as organizing and coordinating systemwide music festivals and events. I was also working with the area music resource teachers in implementing the system's music program, planning and executing meetings of the total music staff, planning in-service courses for systemwide music teachers, and representing the music program at APS school board meetings. It was a huge job, but the many experiences that I had encountered along my journey prepared me for the responsibilities.

As coordinator, I reinstated our All-City Youth Orchestra, continued the annual citywide Marching Band Exhibition, and coordinated citywide music events at the Atlanta Civic Center and at Underground Atlanta.

The Atlanta Public Schools' Fine Arts Festival, held at Underground Atlanta, was comprised of music, art, and physical education (dance). The objective was to showcase students from all levels (elementary, middle, and high school) in a week-long demonstration of our students' talents. The three music supervisors, the supervisory personnel of art and physical education, and I worked for over two months to plan with Underground Atlanta managers. We decided where all of the various groups in each discipline would perform or be displayed (in the area of art).

Projected plans were sent in letters to principals and to teachers in each area. We included a code of conduct for students. The primary rule was that students would not be allowed to roam the huge facility without supervision. The Underground Atlanta personnel were happy to host our festival. They thought that the art exhibition and performances would bring more patrons to their restaurants and shops. We identified approximately twenty venues, both underground and above ground, for the festival. The huge task of assigning groups to the multiple venues in designated time slots proved a daunting task. Another huge task was to schedule buses to pick up groups and return them to their schools. The art supervisors were assigned the task of creating signage that announced each group. A master listing of all activities for each day was my responsibility. Teachers were asked to submit groups for participation with their principals' signature. Each group was allotted a thirty-minute time slot for performances. The art teachers submitted a number of pieces of students' artwork to be displayed. The art supervisors visited schools to check the selections. In music we had bands, orchestras, choruses, hand bells/choir chimes ensembles, and jazz bands to schedule. The all-city bands, choruses, and orchestras were scheduled for the final day and evening. The festival began each day at 10:00 a.m. and ended at 1:30 p.m. The final day's performances began in the morning and resumed in the early evening from 6:00 to 8:00 p.m. When the Monday of the festival arrived, all supervisory personnel arrived at Underground Atlanta at 8:00 a.m. to set up signage and check that risers, music stands, and other needed equipment were in place. The event proved to represent a wonderful public relations vehicle for our school system. Groups were attired in colorful uniforms, and the performances were very enjoyable. The supervisory personnel in each discipline were extremely busy in helping to make the program run smoothly. I think that I did more walking than I had ever experienced in my entire lifetime. Though we had signage at each venue many patrons asked where these students were from. They were high in praise for the many groups and for the extensive art exhibition that was open for the duration of the day.

Huge events like the Underground festival were only one facet of the job. I led the revision of the music curriculum for all levels and served as an advocate and supporter of the arts for the city, state, and nation.

With this leadership position, my professional career began to blossom exponentially. I was called upon to serve as a participant in the Georgia, Southern Division, and National conferences as planner, presenter, or consultant. Involvements in local, regional, and national venues began to evolve.

EXPANDED LOCAL, STATE, AND REGIONAL INVOLVEMENT

Locally, I was involved as a grant panelist for the Fulton County Arts Council and the City of Atlanta Bureau of Cultural Affairs. Additionally, I served on several boards for music-related organizations.

For several years, I presented preconcert lectures for the Atlanta Symphony Orchestra. I was also heavily involved with the orchestra's Audience Development committee, and one of the founders of the Talent Development program.

At the state level, I worked with the Governor's Honors program to select talented music students from across the state. I was involved in elementary and middle school curriculum writing and served as a writer/reviewer for the Georgia Music Teacher Certification Test (TCT). This test, which certified all Georgia music teachers, was under the aegis of the Georgia Assessment Project. It was coordinated by Dr. Donata Renfrow at Georgia State University. I served on several SACS (Southern Association of Colleges and Schools) visiting committees and was a frequent reviewer for the Georgia Professional Practices Commission.

Participation as grant panelist for the Georgia Council for the Arts was truly enjoyable. It involved not only reading and evaluating grants, but also making site visits around the state to evaluate the organizations firsthand.

During this time, I was also one of GMEA's choral and band festival adjudicators. As such, I served as judge for groups around the state. At the Southern Divisional level, I was invited as a panelist for the South Carolina Arts Council for several years and was nominated as one of two candidates for the position of president-elect (another first) for the Southern Division. Though I didn't win the election, I felt that it was quite an honor to have been nominated.

I also had the honor of participating on the Southern Federation Task Force, a strategic planning committee for Southern arts advocacy.

Participating on a regional committee that wrote and published a *Guide for State Music Associations* was very interesting. I appreciated being invited to do this by my former UGA adviser, Dr. James E. Dooley. Many opportunities present themselves by means of connections over time.

Additionally, I served as planner and presenter for several Southern Division conferences. The Southern Division conferences and the National Music conferences met in alternate years. My good friend Dr. Alfred Wyatt and I usually traveled together. I remember conferences in Seattle, Minneapolis, St. Louis, Cincinnati, Phoenix, Atlantic City, Los Angeles, Kansas City, Tampa, Orlando, Chicago, Nashville, Miami, Washington, D.C., New Orleans, and San Antonio, among others. Though I participated in many of these professional events, I also attended the sessions—and improved my skill set over the years. To this day I always encourage young music teachers to become active in the professional organizations and conferences because so much can be learned.

NATIONAL PROFESSIONAL ACTIVITIES

At the national level, I was asked to serve as curriculum writer for the national music standards and the elementary curriculum for MENC/ NAfME.

I also served as grant panelist at the National Endowment for the Arts. I had met Antoinette Handy, a noted musician and author and director of music for the National Endowment, at a music conference. She was apparently impressed with my knowledge of music education and recommended me as a grant panelist for the Endowment. Antoinette Handy became a valued friend. She saw to it that I was involved in numerous national music endeavors.

The Endowment participation truly represented a highlight of my career. I met with several grant panels over the span of ten years. We had the task of evaluating and awarding grants to deserving musical organizations from all over the nation. I learned the importance of networking, of getting to know national leaders in the arts.

I remember that the grant panels met in Washington, D.C., usually over a three-day period. They were held at the landmark Old Post Office (now renovated as the Trump International Hotel). It was a refreshing change of pace to travel to Washington after reading multiple grant applications. The panel members met in the early morning, had lunch together in the lovely downstairs atrium, and then worked feverishly until the evening hours to discuss and evaluate the many grant applications. My only regret was that I never had the time to explore our nation's capital. I always had to return to my job.

PUBLISHING CONSULTANCY

And how excited I was to be invited as Black consultant and writer for the Macmillan McGraw-Hill textbook series *Music and You.* This involvement, too, came about when I met the company's representatives at a national conference. My thesis/special project at UGA had been concerned with the evaluation of current music texts; now I had the opportunity to participate in producing one. I researched and suggested authentic African American songs that were appropriate for each grade level, and I researched artwork by African Americans to enhance pages where the songs were placed. I crafted a synopsis of African American inclusions for the series and listened to proposed recordings of the songs to ensure that arrangements were authentic. I traveled to Florida and other locations for presentations of the textbook series and the African American inclusions. This work took place over a two-year period. After publication, I participated in a revision of the series.

I was also asked to serve on the editorial board of the *Music Educators' National Journal*—a position that I held for four years. Its primary task was to read, evaluate, and recommend acceptance or rejection of submitted articles in the field of music education. The editorial board also presented "how-to sessions on submitting articles." These sessions were held at national conferences. Membership on the board led to an appointment as music adviser for our national organization's *Teaching Music* journal. My role was to answer questions that were submitted by members regarding strategies for teaching music.

I honed my writing skills when I was asked to write essays for the Fisk University Press publication *Notable Black American Men.* This foray into writing resulted in my writing articles for the *American National Biography,* published by Oxford University Press.

In 1990, I was invited by the Getty Center for Education in the Arts to join a national group of participants in Snowbird, Utah. This conference, *Children, the Arts and TV,* was organized to improve the quality of children's television programming for the nation.

The Snowbird ski resort, located near Salt Lake City, sits at an elevation of 11,000 feet. We were warned, in the introductory literature, to avoid drinking any alcoholic beverage before arrival. Doing so would affect us adversely because of the resort's high altitude. But, at the opening reception, the resort served wine! I didn't drink wine, either at home or at the reception. I found the opening conference sessions very interesting. However, near the end of the day, I became quite ill from the unaccustomed high altitude. The next day, I felt much better and was able to rejoin the conference. This experience was special because we were feted with an elaborate barbecue lunch further up the mountain and I had my first ride on a ski lift. We were also transported to an evening performance by the legendary Mormon Tabernacle choir.

My pioneering efforts at UGA prepared me to serve in each of these capacities with confidence and effectiveness. These involvements also broadened my network of nationwide professionals in music education. Meeting many outstanding fellow music educators proved invaluable when I needed to obtain consultants for the music teachers in the Atlanta Public Schools. I always felt that my professional journey was directed by God—not by my own design.

ANOTHER LIFE-CHANGING EVENT

During the 1970s, I had left Mt. Vernon Baptist Church and joined Church of the Master Presbyterian Church. I joined this church so that I could worship with my brother, John, who had also joined the Presbyterian faith. As at Mt. Vernon, I served as church pianist and as a church elder. I have always needed the spiritual nurturance that only a church can provide. That was ingrained in me during early childhood and has never changed.

John passed in 1988. His death affected me deeply because we were very close. I sorely missed his counsel and support as I progressed through my career. I also served as his "listening ear" when he experienced problems.

John had served in the military and attended Howard University for a year in the School of Pharmacy, but decided that this was not the career for him. He returned to Atlanta and studied at the Blayton Business College where he received CPA certification. John thought that he might follow our father's business career, but that didn't work for him either.

He finally joined the Atlanta police force as one of the first African American officers. He worked himself up through the ranks until he was appointed captain. He had just retired from this position before his death. I felt bereft because my parents were deceased and now I had lost my only sibling.

In 1976 I moved from Atlanta to Decatur to a quiet, integrated neighborhood where I learned to enjoy the serenity of my small condominium.

MY ENTHUSIASMS AS A LIFELONG LEARNER

In the middle 1980s, along with twenty-nine other Atlanta Public Schools administrators, I embarked on doctoral studies at Clark Atlanta University. (Atlanta University merged with Clark College in 1988.) We were all working toward an educational leadership doctorate, with dissertations to be completed in our respective fields.

I was excited about this new opportunity for further professional growth, though I would have preferred a doctorate in music education. (Clark Atlanta University did not offer that option.)

We labored for over six years, taking night courses after work and all-day classes on Saturdays. This schedule continued through the summer months. Since we were all annual employees, our schedules remained busy. Summer months meant organizing and coordinating staff development courses for the teachers under our aegis.

It was amazing that we accomplished the huge amount of reading, research projects, and class attendance in addition to the job responsibilities. It was grueling, but interesting, as we learned the cutting-edge strategies of educational leadership.

My good friend Joan Zion and I studied together and passed the comprehensive exam with the highest grades of our cohorts, but we never completed our dissertations. I was too busy working to keep music education a viable curricula component, and Joan, as assistant superintendent for the Elementary Division, had her hands full with the system's reorganization. We were both dedicated to our jobs more than to the distinction of a doctorate.

I registered for dissertation research for six semesters before just giving up on the arduous task of maintaining job responsibilities and writing a major research paper. My adviser told me repeatedly to just write about something in reading or math and do the music research later. I perceived that he was not comfortable with research in music education. I also felt that I would never have the time or the inclination to complete the degree, so I am what is called ABD (All but Dissertation). I had, however, learned much that helped me to serve as a more effective music administrator.

In 1994, I took early retirement from the APS after serving for thirty-seven years. I felt that I had done as much as I could to foster a first-class music program. I needed to pass the torch to someone younger.

Two gala retirement events were held in my honor. The first was planned and hosted by the APS music teachers. It was truly a memorable event. The second was a joint retirement celebration for me and two other APS administrators. Both retirement affairs brought me much joy as I realized that my colleagues felt that I had made a positive contribution to the Atlanta Public Schools.

CHAPTER EIGHT

A Second Career in Higher Education: Expanding My Horizons

———

I truly missed rising in the early morning, working all day, and interacting with others in the profession. Retirement from the job made me realize that while it was time for a change, it wasn't necessarily time for me to sit back and relax. I was still engaged and highly motivated in my professional calling.

So after six months, I accepted an adjunct music position at Morehouse College. Dr. Calvin Grimes, chair of the Music Department, called to ask if I was interested in teaching a Music Appreciation course to nonmusic majors. I knew Calvin Grimes, Uzee Brown, David Morrow, and other Morehouse College professors because I worked with them on the Onyx Opera Board of Directors. (Onyx Opera presented operas by Black composers and served as a performance vehicle for local and nationally known Black vocalists. I coordinated presentations for high school students from the Atlanta Public Schools.) I readily agreed to teach the course at Morehouse. I relished teaching this class because I only needed to plan instruction, teach the class, and correct papers; no administrative tasks, just the actual teaching.

The following year, Dr. Joyce Johnson, department chair, asked me to teach Music Appreciation and Classroom Music at Spelman College, in addition to the course at Morehouse. And then, in 1997, I received a call from Dr. Larry Ervin, dean of Arts and Sciences at Clark Atlanta University (CAU). He told me that his Music Department chairperson was retiring unexpectedly, and that he wanted me to assume the position. I initially declined, but eventually accepted the position with the understanding that I would remain only until another permanent chairperson was hired.

Apparently, they didn't look for another replacement because I worked in that position until 2005.

One pleasant thing that happened while I was at CAU was that I had the opportunity to resume my travels abroad. I traveled with friends Jo-anne Lincoln, Eugene Bales, and Boon Boonyapat to every continent except Antarctica. These international trips usually occurred during CAU's spring break or during the extended Christmas holidays.

Our travel adventures occurred over a period of eighteen years, even after I had retired from CAU. I can't recount each of these experiences but some highlights that remain fresh in my mind include visiting sites that held great power in their natural beauty and their historic qualities. No longer encumbered by the Jim Crow laws of my youth, I was free to see the world and its myriad of cultures. Here are some highlights:

We traveled to Australia and New Zealand in 1999. While watching the sun set at Ayers Rock in Uluru National Park in in Alice Springs, Austra-lia, we were astonished because when the sun sets, the huge mountain turns red and seems to glow from within. It is an awe-inspiring sight.

In Tunisia at age 70 I got to ride a camel in the Sahara Desert. The camel handler assigned me the largest camel of our group. This was a dromedary camel, and it was difficult to ride without rolling from side to side. I experienced great difficulty in mounting and dismounting be-cause the camel was wider in girth than my legs could accommodate. I will never forget the experience of attempting to participate in this ancient form of transportation.

Another memory I have that combined a sense of awe with history was climbing the rocky hill leading to the Parthenon in Athens, Greece. The Parthenon, the most famous building of the Acropolis complex, was built in the fifth century BCE. It stands high above the city of Athens. As I stood in front of this magnificent ancient temple, I thought about its patron goddess, Athena. Years ago, in studying Greek literature, I had learned that Athena was the goddess of wisdom and military victory. I also pondered on her half-brother, Hercules, and her father, Zeus. The interesting stories of Greek mythology had always fascinated me. Now, I was actually in the place of their making, immersed in that rich history.

For more recent history and a painful glimpse into a modern trag-edy, I will never forget viewing the bombed-out homes, schools, and churches in Vukovar, Croatia. My travel group and I were traveling through eastern European countries via a cruise ship. Both Croatia and Serbia were included on our itinerary. When we debarked the ship, we saw a huge white cross just across from where we landed. As our van drove us to the Croatian homes where we were to have lunch, we saw the wide devastation, old tanks, cannons, and other weapons of war. The 40-odd travelers were left at several homes. Our group of four was treated to lunch in a recently renovated, but modest home. After being greeted by our hostess, who didn't speak English, we had the opportunity to hear, firsthand, about the Croatian War of Independence, which began in 1991 and ended in 1995. A young Croatian college student served as our translator. She told us how the Croatians were unaware of an impend-ing attack, and how their homes and buildings were virtually destroyed during the siege by Serbian and Yugoslav forces. The student called the siege the "Vukovar massacre" because hundreds of Croats had been killed. She said that her Serbian schoolmates knew about the impending attack. They failed, however, to warn their Croatian friends. Though the war had ended more than ten years before our 2006 visit, the devastat-ing sights deeply saddened us. They reminded us of the vicious attack on New York City in September 2001. It was indeed a sobering visit to this country with such a rich history and such recent tragedy.

As a lifelong lover of classical music, listening to Mozart's opera *Don Giovanni* in Prague on another trip was an unforgettable experience. As it turned out, our evening had more than just the thrill of the music. We heard the opera at the historic venue where it was premiered. Joanne and I were glad that we were seated at the end of a front row. When the immolation scene was presented, the fire came from a host of live candles. This was a wooden building, and we feared an actual fire, but, fortunately, the music remained the highlight of the evening.

Another somewhat harrowing but beautiful experience was being flown in a small, four-passenger plane over the glaciers in Christchurch, New Zealand. As we were aloft, the pilot informed us that downdrafts surrounding the glaciers often caused planes to crash. This was not very reassuring news to hear as we flew over the glaciers in these magnificent landscapes.

The Christmas of 2013 is one I will always remember with a special sense of awe as we were in the Southern Hemisphere in unusual circumstances. My friends and I actually spent Christmas Day 2013 in three countries: Zimbabwe, Mozambique, and Swaziland, in South Africa. We had spent two days in Swaziland at a lovely hotel. The grounds were overflowing with beautiful, fragrant flowers; the weather was warm and balmy. On Christmas Eve, we decided to request a trip to Zimbabwe and Mozambique on Christmas Day. Though it was not on our itinerary, we had a private driver and travel company and so we could make this request. We paid an additional fee and set off in our luxury van for our excursion. Realizing that this would represent a lengthy trip, we arose early and left at 5:00 a.m. What thrilling sights we saw on our journey! Rolling hills, thickly carpeted plateaus, sparkling waterways, and modern highways captivated us.

The capital city of Maputo was very contemporary. We saw, in Independence Square, a huge statue of a man who represented the Republic of Mozambique being freed from Portuguese rule. Our driver and guide told us about the early history of Mozambique and how it rose to independence with multiparty elections. We stopped at a famous restaurant for lunch. What a delight: truly fresh fish, other seafood, and side dishes provided a fabulous meal. We drove on to Zimbabwe, which was quite a distance. We were astonished at the contrast. This country and the towns that we saw were littered with trash and debris of all types. We were, without a doubt, visiting a Third World country. Poverty seemed a defining factor wherever we went.

Returning on the long ride back to Swaziland, we joined the other guests at the hotel for a traditional Christmas dinner with all the trimmings. Christmas decorations, sparkling white tablecloths, and excellent service from our waitress made the occasion very festive if a little surreal.

I will always be grateful for the opportunity to travel the world. Through my travels, I learned the importance of experiencing firsthand other cultures and awe-inspiring natural sites. They certainly broadened my perspective and respect for the people of the world.

When not on an adventure I continued my work at CAU during these years. I oversaw the move of the department from two portable units to the Park Street Methodist Church building. It had been renovated to accommodate the Music and Art departments of the university. A newly installed elevator provided access to the second and third floors. The Art Department occupied the first floor except for the music library, and the Music Department was housed on the second and third floors. The band room and office were located in the new gym that had been built for the 1996 Olympics in Atlanta.

After getting the Music Department outfitted with furniture and needed equipment, I began to coordinate and implement improvements to the curriculum. I expanded it to include Music Technology (with a computer/keyboard laboratory), World Music, a hand bell ensemble, and several music education courses. All of these courses were added with input from the professors and adjuncts. We met once weekly to discuss important issues with our curriculum. As I reflect on it now, the World Music course was added because my travels had taught me that Western music was not the indigenous music of other countries. We needed to expose students to a broader aspect of the word "music" because they were young adults in a multicultural America.

Clark Atlanta University was far behind in terms of music technology as compared with other universities. I requested and received approval to purchase a ten-station laboratory. Each station was equipped with a computer and a full-size electronic keyboard. They were to be used in music theory courses, music history, and music education.

My experience in developing a hand bell component for the Atlanta Public Schools had convinced me that future music teachers would need to know how to teach these instruments and the music that would be appropriate for all levels. Concomitantly, we needed to expand our music ensembles. Once again, I started by purchasing a set of choir chimes and presented the new ensemble in CAU's annual Christmas concert. President Thomas Cole was so pleased with the ensemble that he asked me how he could help me to improve its goals. I told him that we needed a three-octave set of hand bells. He approved that purchase and the Hand Bell Ensemble assumed an important addition to our high-quality Band, Philharmonic Society, and Jazz Band. The hand bells were also used with each of the music education courses.

I encouraged the chairs of Spelman and Morehouse colleges to join me in developing an Atlanta University Center orchestra. They agreed that this was needed because each of us had string students who had experience with no vehicle to continue their participation. We crafted a job description and with the approval of each president, interviewed prospective orchestra directors. We hired Dr. Alfred Duckett from South Carolina to fill the position. He was paid with contributions from the three schools. Wind and percussion players would be selected from the bands of each school.

CAU offered only one music education course when I assumed the position of chair. It was a composite course. I knew that with an impending SACS review, we needed to expand this course to two separate courses: Elementary Music Methods and Secondary Music Methods. The music professors and I increased the number of music majors and minors. I hired several new professors and adjuncts, revitalized the music alumni participation, and helped to build outstanding marching and concert bands, the chorus or Philharmonic Society, and Jazz Orchestra performance groups.

I had come full circle—beginning my higher education at Clark College as a student, and then returning to lead the Music Department at Clark Atlanta University. This was deeply satisfying. I felt that I was truly giving back to the school that had shaped me in so many ways. After eight years serving as department chair and associate professor at CAU, I took my second retirement in 2005. Unfortunately, the Human Resources Department did not deem my leaving a retirement. They said that I had "quit" and that I had not worked long enough to vest my pension—and so I lost it. I was satisfied, however, because I had done my best to make improvements that would be long-lasting. Also, it was gratifying to know that I had experienced two exciting and rewarding careers *beyond* my desegregation days at UGA, and that through a life of rewarding work, good friends and family, and the opportunities to travel the world, I was living life to its fullest extent regardless of the stultifying effects of the social inequality that plagued my life in the early years.

CAREER HONORS AND POSTRETIREMENT LIFE

During my lengthy career in music education in the Atlanta Public Schools and at Clark Atlanta University, and even afterward, I accrued many honors and awards. Some include: Iota's Bronze Woman of the Year in the Arts; GMEA's Distinguished Award; the Lexus Leader in the Arts from PBA (Public Broadcasting Atlanta); Outstanding Educator Award from the National Black Music Caucus; the Atlanta Freedom's Sisters award hosted by the Jimmy Carter Presidential Library; several awards/proclamations from the mayor of Atlanta, PTAs of Atlanta, and numerous others. Not wanting to bore the reader with an extensive listing, I will merely say that my storage unit in Decatur houses approximately seventy plaques and trophies that were accrued during my professional career. One can find a listing of most of them in my papers at the UGA Russell Library.

After my retirement from Clark Atlanta University, people often asked what I've done to fill my time. Well, I have been very active in my church. I joined the First Christian Church of Decatur—Disciples of Christ—in 1994. I had passed this church many times and, at the time, was still a member of Church of the Master United Presbyterian Church in southwest Atlanta. Living in Decatur, I was quite a distance from that church and was still working on my doctorate. Driving across town on Sundays to attend church became very tiring.

One Sunday, I told my friend Minnie Haynes, who was living with me, that I wanted to go to the First Christian Church just down the street on Ponce de Leon. I told her that we might get kicked out because I knew that the congregation was predominately white.

This was in the month of December and when we went, I was impressed with the warm welcome that we received from congregation members and the minister, the Rev. Robert Boyte.

The church was aglow with candles and lovely Christmas decorations.

A tall, sparkling white Chrismon tree stood behind the altar. The choir and hand bell ensemble performed under the direction of Bob Clarke, the multitalented minister of music.

The sermon by the Rev. Bob Boyte was spiritual and thought-provoking and the service was deeply inspirational. Minnie and I discussed the beauty of the service and the warmth and acceptance of the congregation members.

After visiting the church for several Sundays, Minnie decided to join. I waited about six months before joining. I wanted to be certain that this was the faith community that met my spiritual needs. After making a positive decision, I joined—and in my usual manner, became heavily involved in the church.

I sang in the Chancel choir, participated in the hand bell ensemble, taught children in Vacation Bible School, participated in adult Sunday school, and served as pianist for the early service and for the Gentle Spirit evening service. Participating in the monthly Christian Women's Fellowship (CWF) meetings brought me much joy and satisfaction.

I was elected as an elder and eventually to the chair of elders. I served as vice-moderator and then as moderator of the church. I have also taught the Pathfinders adult Sunday School class and served as pianist for special services and at Sunday services when the regular organist was on vacation. Other church service included Membership Ministry, church trustee, Personnel Ministry, Book Club, coordinator of meals for the annual Christmas tree sale, and serving as a participant in church mission trips.

In addition to church, I have been involved with the Atlanta Symphony Associates (ASA), the support arm for the Atlanta Symphony Orchestra. I was elected vice-chair and then chair of the Concerto unit of the ASA. I served on the Board of Directors as unit chair and head of Community Affairs. For eleven years, I served as preconcert guest lecturer for the symphony concert series. This experience was gratifying and reminded me of my treasured classroom teaching earlier in life.

I helped to initiate the symphony's Talent Development Program. This initiative was designed to level the playing field and bring more diversity to the ASO's Youth Orchestra. It also involved a campaign to develop Black audiences for symphony concerts. I've also volunteered as hostess for the Discover and Symphony Street children's concerts, and coordinated the Target Family Day for the symphony.

As a strong supporter of Atlanta's Symphony Orchestra and member of the Patron Partnership for over thirty years, I have also served as a voice of consciousness in advocating for more diversity within the orchestra. Currently, the ASO has one African American orchestra member, rarely performs symphonic music by Black composers, and even less often invites Black conductors or artists. Sadly, there are very few African Americans on its staff. As a longtime patron of the arts in Atlanta, I cannot help but continue to push for the cause of diversity. Our city has a diverse population and I feel that our world-class orchestra should reflect the entirety of Atlanta.

I do the same for the University of Georgia. I have recruited several outstanding African American students who meet the stringent requirements for admittance. I don't attempt to influence the normal acceptance of students. I just encourage students who possess the academic and other criteria to consider UGA as a viable choice for their higher education.

And then there are the several professional organizations that I attend and am a member: Alpha Chapter of Delta Kappa Gamma Society International for women educators. A twenty-four-year member, I served as president from 1998 to 2000. I am a member also of Sigma Alpha Iota International Music Fraternity (inducted at CAU in 1998 as a Patroness member), as well as the Metropolitan Atlanta Community Band, of which I am a founding member. I now only serve on the Board of Directors, but previously participated as clarinetist, secretary, and grant writer for the board.

I enjoy frequent luncheons with three groups: the Lunch Bunch, comprised of retired APS administrators, which meets monthly; also, the Coan group, including retired teachers and administrators from Coan Middle School; and the APS Retired Music Teachers group that meets for lunch and plans strategies to advocate for a stronger APS music curriculum. Add to that schedule the subscription concerts at Symphony

Hall, the Emory Schwartz Center concerts, and several other cultural events. One can readily see how busy I am still—even as an octogenarian. This is also an indication of how rich music and music education have made my life, on so many levels.

Since reconciliation with the University of Georgia I have made many trips to Athens. The official visits are described in the next chapter, but others were more personal in nature. I went to Athens in April 2017 to view the screening of the documentary *Athens in Our Lifetime: Recalling the Evolution of Our Town over the Past Six Decades*. I was among the ninety participants who were interviewed for this historic documentary. It was produced by H. Grady Thrasher and his wife, Kathy Prescott. This first showing at the Ciné Theater had a full-capacity audience. Additional showings attracted over 2,000 patrons. Other screenings included one for the OLLI series, another at the Georgia Museum of Art at UGA, and several others.

In October 2018, I returned to UGA for what has become a tradition for me. I attended the UGA homecoming game. As guests of President Morehead, my companion and I were seated in the president's Sky suite. What a treat! We were not only delighted to experience UGA's triumphant win over Missouri, I was able to enjoy the outstanding UGA Redcoat band—joined by an impressive Alumni band.

Add to those trips a November visit to the Watkinsville home of Grady Thrasher and Kathy Prescott, called Sunnybank Farm. Grady is a lawyer and a strong supporter of recording and interpreting Athens history. He is also a noted author and a budding artist. His wife, Kathy, is a very talented artist. Betty Williford, my wonderful friend, accompanied me on this visit. We were driven by Greg Morrison, who was going to get some video segments from Grady and his video producer, Matt DeGennaro. Betty and I enjoyed the drive to Watkinsville. The November weather was perfect—a sunny day with blue clouds overhead. As our car drove up the winding road to the farm, we saw a lovely white house with a barn to the left. We were greeted by Grady and Kathy as we admired the beautiful interior of the house. Over lively conversation, Kathy served us a lavish lunch of delicacies that she had prepared. When we went outside, we saw that the barn included a tube slide from the top floor to the ground. Grady said that it was used by their grandchildren in their youthful years. I could easily imagine gleeful children sliding down the chute, then running back upstairs to slide once again.

I noticed a swing that was tethered to a tall tree. I walked over to it and thought back to my childhood when we had a similar swing in our backyard. I just had to try this wonderful experience again! I hopped into the swing, held onto both ropes very tightly, started the swing with my feet and soared into the crisp air. What freedom I felt as the swing moved back and forth—higher and higher! My thoughts went back to the days when I taught my John Hope chorus an arrangement of Robert Louis Stevenson's lyrics to "The Swing": *Up in the air I go flying again, Up in the air and down!*" I was completely unaware that both Grady and Greg were taking photos of me as I swung. Later they presented me with a framed copy of me in the swing. My broad smile was both gleeful and reflective.

Following this adventure, we all went into the barn and caught up with Matt and Kathy. The first floor of the barn held Grady's studio. The walls held a gallery of Kathy's lovely artwork. Greg remained in the studio with Matt, and the rest of us walked outside to view the beautiful lake that reflected the majestic trees and everything around it. This visit with these creative people made me feel part of the important narrative we need to tell about Athens and its evolution.

CHAPTER NINE

Reconciliation with UGA

Q uite unexpectedly, the University of Georgia came back into my life before I left Clark Atlanta University.

In 1997, I received a phone call from Dr. Maurice Daniels, then professor at UGA's School of Social Work. (Dr. Daniels was later promoted to the office of dean.)

He told me that he was working on a documentary about Horace T. Ward, the first African American to apply to UGA. Daniels said that he had interviewed attorney Donald Hollowell, who was the chief counsel for the Hunter/Holmes court case. He had also interviewed Mr. Jesse Hill Jr. and Vernon Jordan. Both Hollowell and Hill had told him that Mary Frances Early was the first African American to receive a degree from UGA.

Dr. Daniels was calling to verify this startling information. During his years at UGA, he had never heard my name in connection with the 1961 desegregation. I told him that this was indeed true. I *was* the first African American to receive a degree at UGA. Since this was new information, Dr. Daniels researched this revelation and substantiated it. Shortly afterward, I was asked to attend a videotaping at Georgia State University. Daniels interviewed me as part of the documentary's second segment. It was entitled *Foot Soldier for Equal Justice,* and featured Horace T. Ward's attempts to integrate UGA's Law School. It also depicted his later triumphs in assisting Hollowell in the successful verdict of *Holmes v. Danner,* the case that settled the question of whether Charlayne and Hamilton could attend UGA. Both Charlayne and Hamilton were also featured in the documentary.

In 2000, I received an invitation from Tracey Ford, graduate assistant to Dr. Daniels, and Valerie White, a GAPS student, to come to UGA and serve as guest speaker for the Graduate and Professional Scholars' (GAPS) annual lecture. I was asked to speak about my experiences at UGA.

I wondered, initially: "Do I really want to return to the UGA campus after being ignored for over thirty years?" The invitation brought back hurtful memories that I had hidden in the recesses of my mind and heart. I had taken personal affront that my alma mater had essentially erased me from its history. UGA's stance regarding me had resulted in the Atlanta media also ignoring my role in its desegregation. I was not mentioned when articles regarding the fortieth and fiftieth anniversaries of UGA's desegregation were printed. How does an institution ignore someone who had been the first person of color to obtain a degree? As a consequence, people in Atlanta had consistently asked me if I really was the first Black to receive a degree. This made me feel devalued. I had brought no dishonor to UGA, Atlanta, or Georgia.

I have always wanted to know the reasons for this unfair treatment, but have never found an answer. The hurt feelings that I had suppressed for so long returned. But then I thought: "Yes, I *do* want to return. I need to tell my story because it's part of UGA's history."

I agreed to visit the campus and to serve as guest speaker. Arrangements were made, the date set, and I returned to UGA with my friend Darlyne Killian and her granddaughter on April 18, 2000. The event was held at the Law School building and was attended by a capacity audience. Obviously, people were curious about this story that had never been told. I was proud of the fact that my family, minister, several church members, and friends were able to attend.

After introductory remarks, the *Foot Soldier* documentary segment that included my story was shown. And then it was my turn to speak. I had titled my speech "Integrating the University of Georgia: The Early Years" (meaning my name). I spoke of my experiences without rancor or bitterness; I simply told the story.

After the speech, I was presented with a proclamation from President Michael F. Adams confirming the fact that I was UGA's first Black student to receive a degree. I felt so validated, so relieved that at last my role in UGA's desegregation had been publicly acknowledged—at least on campus. It was very gratifying.

The GAPS president, Jessica DeCuir, announced that the lecture was being renamed in my honor. My minister, the Rev. Dr. James Brewer-Calvert, presented me with a lovely bouquet of roses.

At the reception that followed, I was overwhelmed with congratulations from the graduate students, UGA faculty and staff members, family and friends. It was a true mountaintop experience. Who says that one can't go back home again?

After the lecture in 2000, my relationship with UGA changed dramatically. The lecture in my name has continued now for over twenty years. Outstanding guest speakers including Congressman John Lewis, former ambassador Andrew Young, Cynthia Tucker, Donna Brazile, Hank Klibanoff, Maurice Daniels, Michael Thurmond, Johnetta Cole, former surgeon general Jocelyn Elders, and Bakari Sellers have served as keynote speakers.

The Graduate School and Office of Institutional Diversity have joined GAPS as co-sponsors. The Office of the President, Alumni Association, School of Social Work, and other campus organizations also assist in sponsoring this annual event.

I became quite active with UGA, serving on the Alumni Association's Board of Directors, the Graduate School's Graduate Education Advancement Board, and more recently, the College of Education's Board of Visitors; speaking on multiple occasions on and off campus, and attending many events including homecoming games as a guest of the president.

A professorship in my name was initiated by the College of Education with $250,000 donated by the Georgia Power Company as seed money. In 2012 Dr. Cynthia Dillard was appointed as the first Mary Frances Early Professor of Education. I felt deeply honored because Dr. Dillard is a brilliant author, professor, and Educational Theory and Practice Department chair. In 2007, following a Diversity Days celebration program, my portrait and those of Charlayne Hunter-Gault and Hamilton Holmes were unveiled in the Academic building. Diversity Days represents an annual event that is sponsored by the Office of Institutional Diversity at UGA.

Also in 2007, I was asked by the then Graduate School dean, Dr. Maureen Grasso, to serve as commencement speaker for the Graduate School. This was a signal honor and I remembered that Charlayne Hunter-Gault had served as undergraduate commencement speaker as early as 1988. I spoke to 1,000-plus graduate students, their families, friends, and UGA administrators.

My address was entitled "Roots and Wings." I told the graduates that I wished them roots so that they would never forget where they started . . . and wings so that they might reach whatever heights to which they aspired. Vernon Jordan, the civil rights activist and attorney who worked with Donald Hollowell, received an honorary doctorate during the undergraduate ceremony. He had played a major role in the *Holmes v. Danner* court case.

In 2010, a tree planting ceremony was held on the campus of the School of Music. The Graduate School planted a pink dogwood tree in my honor. A bronze plaque marked the honor alongside the tree. I had never participated in a tree planting before, and this was a new and very special experience. A lovely reception was held in the Georgia Museum of Art afterward.

In January 2011, UGA hosted the fiftieth anniversary of its desegregation in a week-long celebration. Dr. Cheryl Dozier, associate provost and director of the Office of Institutional Diversity, and Dr. Derrick Alridge, director of the Institute for African American Studies, served as co-chairs for this momentous event. The theme of the fiftieth anniversary was "Celebrating Courage." On Sunday evening, a gala opening session was held at the UGA Conference Center. A capacity, diverse audience attended. Honorees included Charlayne Hunter-Gault and her husband; Marilyn Holmes, wife of the late Dr. Hamilton Holmes; Louise Hollowell, wife of the late attorney Donald Hollowell; and me.

On the next day, however, the weather turned inclement with ice and snow. Charlayne Hunter-Gault delivered the fiftieth anniversary address. A few other sessions followed, including one where Charlayne signed over her papers to UGA.

The evening session featured Dr. Daniels's documentary on Donald Hollowell. Mrs. Hollowell spoke about her husband, and I made remarks about how he had assisted me during my time at UGA. The week-long celebration was postponed after that evening session because the icy roads and streets prevented others from attending. Our entire gathering of speakers and guests was snowbound for three days at the Conference Center where we were housed.

I was scheduled to deliver the keynote address for the Friday Freedom Breakfast honoring Dr. Martin Luther King Jr. Unfortunately, the breakfast was also postponed until February 14. On that day, I spoke to a capacity crowd of 600 at 7:30 in the morning! I was humbled to have the opportunity to speak about my hero, Dr. Martin Luther King Jr. This was truly a highlight of my life because he had been such an inspiration as I confronted inequality and injustice and because I had known him personally when he was leading the charge in the 1960s. Since February 14 was Valentine's Day, I rewrote my speech to focus on Dr. King's theme of love for all people. I even sang "What the World Needs Now Is Love Sweet Love." I hadn't planned to sing; it was just a spontaneous affirmation of how I felt at the moment.

In August 2012, UGA honored me with a commemorative event recognizing the fiftieth anniversary of my receiving the first degree. This event was held in the newly renovated auditorium of the Fine Arts building. This was the venue where I had received my degree fifty years before. I felt so blessed to be able to celebrate a golden anniversary of my first UGA degree. Family, friends, as well as UGA students, administrators, faculty, and staff were in attendance. I even had a van-load of classmates from Clark College in attendance. Several of my church's members also attended this prestigious event. I am fortunate to have such loyal members of my faith community. They support me on so many occasions.

Lonnie King, leader of the Atlanta Student Movement and also an elementary school classmate at E. P. Johnson School, served as keynote speaker. It was indeed a grand occasion. Tributes and presentations from so many marked the event: a proclamation from President Michael F. Adams; a scholarship in my name from the Hodgson School of Music; a Martin Luther King Jr. plaque from the College of Education; a book plaque from the Alumni Association; a memory book from the Office of

Institutional Diversity; a crystal sculpture from my Clark College class-mates; and a plaque from Clark Atlanta University. This event was truly awe-inspiring. A magnificent reception followed the program. I enjoyed connecting with many people I had met along my journey.

And then in 2013, the greatest tribute that UGA could grant. I was awarded an honorary doctor of laws degree at the spring undergraduate commencement.

My retina specialist had just diagnosed me with severe macular de-generation in my right eye. This was devastating news because I had already lost central vision in my left eye in 2007. Dr. Hendrick told me that he could immediately begin a series of eye injections that would slow the progress of my condition. He said that I would probably not feel well, and that my eye would be very red. I told him that I would wait until after the UGA event. I liked the colors of red and black, but I didn't want a red eye for this important occasion.

The ceremony, however, was so special that I almost forgot that I would have to begin a series of eye injections at the Emory Eye Clinic the following week.

I went to campus the day before commencement because I had been asked to serve as convocation speaker for the College of Education's graduating students. Following my arrival on campus, I received a call from my minister. He sounded excited as he told me that he'd just read an article in the *Atlanta Journal-Constitution*. It was about my UGA his-tory and the honorary degree that I was to receive. I hadn't seen the newspaper, but remembered that Bo Emerson, AJC journalist, had in-terviewed me the previous week and had had photos taken at my home. I was so glad that my hometown newspaper had finally, after fifty-one years of silence, reported to Atlanta about my role in UGA's history. This article also alerted many old friends and colleagues of the struggle and accomplishments I lived through. Bill Dyson, who served on the GMEA board at my encouragement and was orchestra director for the Atlanta Public Schools when I was in charge, wrote to congratulate me, saying that he had never known of the challenges I was faced with at UGA. He said reading the article made my career and leadership in the Atlanta Public Schools all the more significant to him. "A generation of students in Atlanta has been served to the maximum because of your influence on their music education," he wrote.

I am deeply indebted to Hank Klibanoff, the 2013 Mary Frances Early guest lecturer, for that AJC article. Though he never claimed credit, I believe that his past positions with the paper, and his influence, led to the article.

I spoke for the College of Education convocation spontaneously because I could no longer see any notes. My address was well received by the graduates and their families and I was grateful for their enthusiasm. The next morning, I attended the graduate commencement and then attended a special luncheon hosted by President Adams. The luncheon honored the two commencement speakers.

My friend Minnie Haynes had driven me to Athens and she was excited because one of her granddaughters, Carmin Haynes, was receiving her undergraduate degree that evening. We gathered in the "green room" for a buffet dinner just before the commencement. My aunt Geneva Locklin and her daughter Sandra Kay Locklin had been invited to the dinner. They also had reserved seats for the commencement ceremony in Sanford Stadium.

After robing, the dignitaries, administrators, and faculty formed the processional line. We entered the stadium, which was crowded with 5,000 undergraduates, along with their families and friends. When I marched into the stadium and saw the huge crowd of students and audience, I was completely overwhelmed. When I thought back to my commencement fifty-one years earlier, I asked myself: "Is this really happening?" Could I have ever possibly imagined this event on that day back in 1962?

Senator Saxby Chambliss served as the commencement speaker, and a brilliant graduating student delivered the valedictory. Following the speeches, Dr. Adams announced my honorary doctorate. Dr. Maurice Daniels, my "discoverer," and Mr. Jere Morehead, current president of UGA, draped me with the hood signifying the honor.

At the point when I made a brief response, I could hardly speak! The entire audience and graduating students gave me a standing ovation. I have never felt prouder and wished that my parents had been there to witness my honor. They were, after all, largely responsible for any successes that I had attained.

The diploma was quite large with elegant framing. It was too heavy for me to carry from the stage. Dr. Daniels graciously carried it for me.

This ceremony marked Dr. Adams's final commencement as president of UGA. The event honored him with a commissioned composition performed by the UGA orchestra. An exciting display of fireworks followed the recessional. It was indeed a night to remember.

The following week, I was honored by my first alma mater: Clark College/Clark Atlanta University. A lavish banquet was held at the Hyatt Regency Hotel in Atlanta. The university was recognizing its Pathways to Excellence alumni, and I was included among the five honorees.

After dinner, a video of each honoree was shown to the audience (we had all been interviewed and videotaped previously). After each video, the honoree was escorted to the stage and presented with a marble-based trophy. We also received a huge framed collective portrait of all the honorees. I was humbled and deeply moved to receive yet another outstanding award.

Though I don't travel to UGA as frequently as I once did, I am still there as often as my physical self can manage. I have lost the ability to drive because of my macular degeneration—and sometimes it is not possible to find a driver. That loss of independence has made a marked impact on my life.

During 2017, I did travel to UGA in January. I was there to reconnect with the first three freshmen—Mary Blackwell Diallo, Kerry Rushin Miller, and Harold Black—who were the first Black students to spend four years and receive degrees. They were being honored by UGA in a special evening program and at the annual Freedom Breakfast. Charlayne Hunter-Gault was there to interview them for the Russell Library archives. It was so good to see them and to have the first three set of Black degree recipients together for the first time!

As though these recognitions were not enough, I was honored by the UGA Graduate School in Athens in October 2017. I was named among nine recipients for the Alumni of Distinction award. The awards ceremony followed an elaborate banquet held at the Russell Library. I did so enjoy hearing the contributions of the other recipients. Dean Suzanne Barbour introduced each one and made the presentations. The names of recipients since the year 2013 were listed in the printed program. I felt honored to be included among so many outstanding graduate alumni.

I had thought that the honorary degree represented the most prestigious award that UGA could confer. It had been approved by the Board of Regents and presented by President Emeritus Michael F. Adams. In January 2018, however, I was honored with the esteemed President's Medal, awarded by President Jere Morehead. This award, presented to two faculty/alumni each year, was so special. The 2018 President's Medals were presented to Delmer "Dell" Dunn and to me. Recipients are chosen by the UGA Emeriti Scholars and the Alumni Association. This year's presentation was held in January during the Founders' Week luncheon. Several of my family members and friends were in attendance.

The lovely bronze medal with black ribbon is breathtaking; both sides of the medal are engraved with historical symbolism of UGA's past, and one side bears the recipient's name. I was so impressed with this beautiful medal that I had it placed in a professional shadow box for all to see.

CONTINUING WITH THE
FOOT SOLDIER FILM BRIGADE

In January 2017, interviews for another *Foot Soldier* documentary began. I was astonished to learn that Dr. Maurice Daniels was producing yet another documentary and this one was featuring me. It was co-produced by Dr. Daniels and Dr. Michelle Cook, Vice Provost for Diversity and Inclusion. Greg Morrison and his companion LaGeris Bell interviewed a former student, Lance Jackson, Lonnie King, my very close friend Betty Williford, Dr. Juanita Johnson-Bailey, me, and others. The documentary premiered on September 11, 2018, and Monica Kaufmann Pearson served as narrator. She also interviewed me following the screening. The screening was held at the Georgia Power headquarters building in Atlanta and was attended by a capacity audience. The location was especially meaningful for me as the Georgia Power Company had also generously initiated the Mary Frances Early professorship at UGA. Guests at the event enjoyed a sumptuous reception before the screening and I was able to meet and greet many of the attendees. The documentary also aired on Georgia Public Television several times following the initial screening.

A UGA campus screening was held in February 2019 at the Tate Student Center. This event was part of UGA's Black History Month celebration and was sponsored by the Office of Institutional Diversity, the College of Education, the Graduate School, Graduate and Professional Scholars, the Office of the Dean of Students, the Tate Student Center, and the Institute of Higher Education. Again, a lovely reception preceded the screening. I was delighted to meet many attendees including Dr. Michael Adams, president emeritus of UGA, who was the first UGA president to recognize my role in the university's desegregation.

In February 2018, Fox 5 News televised a brief Black History sketch about me. Aungelique Proctor, noted journalist and reporter, interviewed me and narrated the segment. This event is significant because this was the first time that I had been featured on television during Black History month. The sparse media attention to my role in UGA's desegregation history was being addressed. In 2019, I was interviewed on Georgia Public Broadcasting radio by Virginia Prescott, host of *On Second Thought*. This was followed by a WABE radio interview by Rose Scott on her program *A Closer Look with Rose Scott*. And then a *People to People* interview with Condace Pressley on WSB television. Perhaps now fewer Atlanta citizens would ask me if I was truly the first Black to receive a UGA degree.

Another outstanding honor I received that year was the commission and hanging of my official portrait in the gallery outside of the president's office in the UGA Administration Building. The portrait was initiated with a suggestion by UGA Graduate School dean Suzanne Barbour. She introduced me to the highly talented, nationally acclaimed artist Richard Wilson from North Carolina. The project was continued by the president's office and in a few months, after an extended photo shoot of me, the portrait was completed. An unveiling ceremony was held in the Administration Building in October 2018. I was pleased that my longtime friend and Atlanta Public Schools colleague Cynthia Terry accompanied me to Athens for the ceremony. It was attended by many UGA administrators, faculty, friends, and students. President Morehead and I did the unveiling. I had not seen the official portrait until that moment during the ceremony and I was very pleased with the superb work of the artist, who was also present. A lively reception followed the unveiling. The portrait was placed on the wall in a prestigious location by two strong UGA workers. I took many photos beside the portrait with my cousin James Locklin, the artist Richard Wilson, Dean Suzanne Barbour, Dean Emeritus Maurice Daniels, and the Mary Frances Early Professor, Dr. Cynthia Dillard, with several friends and students, and of course with President Morehead.

January 2019 presented another challenge for me. Though I had scaled back my speaking engagements, this one was part of a celebration of Dr. Martin Luther King Week and was one that I couldn't refuse. I had been contacted by Dr. Pamela Whitten, former provost at UGA and subsequently president of Kennesaw State University, in November and asked to speak at the King Week event at Kennesaw. I agreed because it was initially meant to feature a screening of the documentary *Mary Frances Early: The Quiet Trailblazer*. The plan was that Dr. Maurice Daniels and I would be interviewed and respond to questions from the students and other audience members. Unfortunately, Dr. Daniels was scheduled to have surgery in January, and so the format was changed to a keynote speech by me. As mentioned before, Dr. King was my hero; second, I couldn't refuse an invitation from Dr. Whitten. She was always very supportive of me and attended every event in which I was involved at UGA.

My central vision had deteriorated to the point that I had to resort to memorizing the sequence of points that I wanted to say. This I did and was driven to Kennesaw State University for the event. I was amazed with the growth of the Kennesaw campus. Several new and impressive buildings with lovely green spaces now enhance the growing campus. I remembered a visit to Kennesaw while I was still working when I participated in a SACS review, and the campus was not nearly that expansive. I enjoyed talking with President Whitten as we walked to the venue where the event was held. I noted the friendliness of the students as we rode on an elevator to the space where the program was being held. This was a luncheon meeting of faculty, students, and staff, and the room was very crowded. The program began just after we entered—and quickly I was on stage to speak. The audience was very engaged with my speech; afterward, I enjoyed meeting with a smaller group of students. I listened to them describe their experience at Kennesaw and was quite impressed with their enthusiasm. I considered as I was being driven home that Kennesaw State University has grown significantly over the years and is on target to be one of the largest schools in the State University System of Georgia.

It was difficult to believe that twenty years had elapsed since I returned to the UGA campus in 2000. The annual Mary Frances Early Lecture was held on March 26, 2019, at the Georgia Center for Continuing Education. Candace Haynes, Minnie's second granddaughter and a UGA alumna, drove us to Athens a day before the lecture.

I always meet with the GAPS (Graduate and Professional Scholars) the day preceding the lecture. This wonderful group of UGA minority students represent the initiators of the lecture in my name. This meeting began as a coffee hour, but has progressed to a full dinner meeting. This year's dinner meeting was held at the UGA Conference Center where Minnie, Candace, and I were housed. After the meal I ask the GAPS students to introduce themselves and to tell me about where they are from, their major field of study, and the degree they are seeking. I wanted this information because the group is fluid in composition. Some students have received their degrees and left UGA; others were not part of the previous year's group. I also ask about how they are doing in their studies and problems they are experiencing. I always encourage them and offer any words of wisdom that seem appropriate.

The 2019 dinner was an elegant buffet of delicious food. We ate and then began our discussion. Others who are not part of the group were present: Vanessa Smith, who works with the Office of Institutional Diversity, and Broderick Flanagan with his wife. Broderick, a local talented visual artist, attended a GAPS dinner four years ago. He came to present to me a portrait of me that he had painted. The portrait is beautiful and remains one of my treasured possessions. I had not known Broderick before his presentation, but have followed him in his career as an artist. His studio is located in Athens and he is recognized as a talented son of Athens. At the dinner I also introduced Minnie and Candace and asked them to give words of encouragement to the GAPS students.

The following day, we attended the luncheon that is always held in my honor. I met the speaker, Dr. Christopher Emdin. Dr. Emdin is an associate professor in mathematics, science, and technology at Teachers College, Columbia University, New York. Our conversation was animated and interesting. After the luncheon, we had a photo session with Nancy Evelyn, photographer for the UGA Graduate School. Following this, we had a chance to continue our conversation that began at the luncheon. I found Dr. Emdin to be gracious and compelling in his passion for contemporary educational strategies.

The lecture began with a warm welcome by Ashley Love, president of GAPS. President Jere Morehead offered additional words of welcome and remarks regarding the lecture. When Dr. Emdin was introduced and took the stage, he delivered a riveting and animated lecture. The audience responded with thunderous applause. I spoke to the audience briefly and the program ended with closing remarks by Dr. Michelle Cook, who not only serves as vice-provost of diversity, but also as leader of Strategic University Initiatives.

At the reception that followed, I shook hands with and took photos with many of the audience members and friends. I had been told that I needed to conclude my greetings before 5:00 p.m. as we were to be transported to the administration building for a photo session with family members beside my portrait. I managed to do this. My family, generally cousins, and I were driven in a van and some cars, but instead of going to the administration building we were taken to the back of the UGA chapel. I asked Arthur Tripp, the efficient assistant to the president, why we were stopping there. He told me that I had mentioned the year before that I had a dream of ringing the chapel bell but had never done so. He said that this dream was about to be realized.

I was so amazed and pleased that my dream was about to come true. I was also nervous because I didn't know if I could manage to ring that bell. Like the university's famous arches, the chapel bell represents a symbol of victory. It is usually rung by a student after UGA had a victorious football game. I certainly had many victories to celebrate, but was uncertain how this would go. My cousins Minnie and Candace were standing on the sidewalk below. There were several photographers on the ledge that held the chapel bell. Could I, an 82-year-old with osteoporosis, ring the bell? My climb up the steps to the bell was tentative but sure. President Morehead was standing on the ledge smiling at me. I returned his smile and took hold of the rope that rang the bell. I pulled once and then again. Nothing happened. I was embarrassed by my failure. President Morehead walked over and said that he would assist me in ringing the bell. We pulled—and the bell rang! I thanked him and said, "But I've got to do this myself." He stepped back; I looked up the high shaft that held the bell, whispered a prayer, bent my knees, and tugged. And the bell rang. I extended both arms in a joyful victory as the viewers and President Morehead applauded. The photographers had been snapping photos all along. The one that resulted from this victory pose went viral over many publications. I took photos with my cousins Sandra Kaye and her adult children, Patrice and Patrick. I also took a photo with Candace. This was a remarkable experience for me—one that I will never forget.

Memories of Langston Hughes's poem "A Dream Deferred" entered my mind. It had inspired the noted playwright Lorraine Hansberry to write her well-known play *A Raisin in the Sun*, which was the first play by an African American to be produced on Broadway. *"What happens to a dream deferred? Does it dry up like a raisin in the sun?"* wrote Langston Hughes. Well, my dream was not deferred. Thanks to my wonderful friends at UGA, my dream became a reality.

Afterward we went to the administration building and I took several photos with my supportive cousins and with Minnie, her son Darryl and his wife Evoni, and with Candace, his daughter. The 2019 lecture and its activities, especially the surprise trip to the chapel bell, will be long remembered.

Back in Atlanta and five days later I was honored by the Henry McNeal Turner High School National Alumni Association. Turner High had opened in September 1951 as Atlanta's premier Black high school. Sadly, Turner closed as a high school in 1990. The Atlanta Public Schools had instituted the middle school concept and so Turner was reopened as a middle school. This school closed in 2016 because of declining enrollment. The building now houses KIPPS Academy—a charter school.

In 2002 the Turner High National Alumni Association was formed. An annual prayer breakfast was begun with alumni attending in large numbers. Several other activities are held throughout the year. The annual prayer breakfast raises funds to sponsor scholarships for academically talented high school students in the metro Atlanta schools. The breakfast always features a noted alumni speaker from one of the thirty-eight classes that graduated and I had been the speaker for this event in 2004. The 2019 event was held on Saturday, March 30. Dorothy T. Swann, president, informed me earlier that I would be honored at this event.

The Georgia International Convention Center is located in College Park, close to the Hartsfield-Jackson Airport. A huge and imposing venue, the center accommodates large numbers of attendees. The 2019 breakfast was attended by over 1,700 alumni from all over the nation. (It is truly a sight to see as these alumni come attired in the school colors—green and white.) Former faculty and staff members are included in that number and are seated at special tables and recognized during the program. The "golden" class for each year is celebrated during the program. This year, the class of 1969 was recognized. Each member who is present has his or her name called as the class members process down the center aisle to seats. The speakers for this event, Clarence Robie and Rev. Nawanna Miller, were also from the Class of 1969.

My recognition occurred near the beginning of the program. I was escorted down the central aisle by a fellow member of the class of 1953: the Rev. Dr. W. N. Freeman. The president, Dorothy T. Swann, introduced me to the audience and presented me with a large bouquet of white roses adorned with a green ribbon. She also presented a lovely plaque from the Alumni Association. The large audience stood and sang the Turner High alma mater—written by me as an eleventh-grader. Jean Blackshear Harris, our class salutatorian, led the singing. The beautiful souvenir program featured a photo of me when I served as speaker in

2004, several pages of biography, and pages with more recent photos. It felt so good to be so acknowledged by my high school alumni friends, one former Turner principal, faculty and staff members. As a life member of the association, I continue to support my former high school. I feel a special fondness and bond with this school that helped to shape my life and career.

A lasting honor also arrived in 2019 when I was informed that an initiative had been launched to name the College of Education in my honor. I learned about this when Dr. Denise Spangler, UGA's dean of the College of Education, and Arthur Tripp, assistant to the UGA president, visited my home. Mr. Tripp said that President Morehead wanted to join in the conversation. He called him and pressed the speakerphone icon. When President Morehead came on the phone he told me the purpose of the call and said that he wanted the news to be delivered in person because of its importance. His message was that the College of Education would be named in my honor. I sat and listened with disbelief! Never in my wildest dreams had I imagined that something of this magnitude would happen to me. I was almost speechless—but managed to stammer out a sincere "thank-you." Dean Spangler and Arthur Tripp talked with me after the phone conversation ended. They explained that the honor would include a gift of one million dollars and then approval from the Georgia Board of Regents. They said that President Morehead had seeded $200,000 of the needed amount and that the University Foundation would match his gift. The money would be used for needs-based scholarships for undergraduate students in the College of Education and music education students from the Hodgson School of Music. This fact gave me much satisfaction. I am a firm believer in education as the path to one's success. Knowing that the money would be allocated to students who would pursue a degree in this area made my joy complete.

Later that month, I traveled to Athens for a two-day visit. My schedule was crowded with many things that I needed to do: a meeting with Dean Spangler to discuss the honor and the path forward; a retirement event for Vanessa Smith for her dedicated work in the Office of Institutional Diversity; an OLLI session with my hostess—Joan Zitzelman; a meeting with my editor, who is based in Athens; and three meal functions with friends who live in Athens. These visits remind me of what long and deep connections I have to the university.

In June, an elaborate reception was held in Atlanta at the elegant Buckhead Club on Peachtree Street. It was sponsored by the College of Education and attended by friends, students that I had taught many years ago, former teachers, co-workers, and administrators, and others that I did not know. Presidents of the Atlanta Symphony Associates with whom I had worked to support the Atlanta Symphony Orchestra were there and many more. They were invited to hear about the honor that I was receiving and how they could support it. It was a lovely affair with food, drinks, and lively conversation. This was indeed an exciting evening.

Four months later, I traveled to Ireland with my cousin Ray Clark and his wife, Carol Grabauskas, for a twelve-day trip. I hadn't traveled abroad since 2013–2014 because my rapidly declining vision made traveling so difficult. My cousins promised to serve as my vision helpers and I was super excited to travel to a country that I'd never visited. Little did I know that this trip would provide much more than just travel adventures. We flew to Dublin and spent some lovely days there. I was so impressed with the verdant flora, nurtured by the intermittent rains and the varying landscapes. Ray had rented a luxury BMW SUV in which he capably drove us to all of our destinations. We left Dublin for Galway. Ray's daughter Tamala had flown from her home in Austria to join us. We had fun viewing the sites, shopping for souvenirs, and eating at fine restaurants. While dining in a lovely restaurant on the evening of October 16, I received a text message from President Morehead. I couldn't read the small print but Carol read it for me. President Morehead wanted me to know that the million dollars had been raised two months earlier than the December deadline. He wrote that the College of Education naming initiative had been submitted to the Georgia Board of Regents and approved by the board on that day. He was aware that I was traveling and wanted me to hear the news first from him. Words are inadequate to describe my excitement as Carol read the text message! We celebrated with a wonderful steak dinner complete with an expensive champagne and delectable desserts. The wait staff joined in the celebration because they had heard our excitement and wanted to join in the fun. Needless to say, we had excellent service throughout our dinner and I felt like royalty.

The four of us rode on to Limerick and then to Gorey where Tamala's son and Ray's grandson joined us. We enjoyed a family dinner at Tamala's family home. Our trip progressed to more sights as we visited castles and gardens, museums, and the world-famous Cliffs of Moher. Our final destination before returning to Dublin was Portmarnock where we enjoyed staying in a luxury hotel. I loved the sights of the Irish Sea with its rolling blue waters. We journeyed back to Dublin for a final dinner of its famous fish and chips. I passed on the foamy Guinness beer but I had thoroughly enjoyed my trip to the Emerald Isles.

When I returned home, my life took on a frenetic pace. Innumerable phone calls, emails, invitations to events and to UGA became overwhelming. I asked Candace Haynes, my friend Minnie's granddaughter, to serve as my personal assistant for a small fee. I needed help. She assisted with phone calls and correspondence and drove me to Athens for meetings and to Georgia Public Broadcasting for an interview. I was asked by the College of Education to provide memorabilia for display and photo albums to display on walls. We also traveled to Athens for a meeting with my editor at the Russell Library, for interviews at COE, and to a luncheon meeting with the Eta Xi campus AKA chapter. Add to that the usual tasks of paying bills, purchasing groceries, cooking, and other household tasks and one can see how busy my life was at that point.

This rather prolonged prelude to the February celebratory events also included a recognition by the Atlanta Symphony at a Talent Development recital; a presentation by the Atlanta City Council; a presentation by the Atlanta Public Schools' superintendent, Dr. Maria Carstarphen; and a Lifetime Achievement Award by GMEA at its January conference.

The February celebratory events at UGA in Athens were scheduled for a two-day period: February 24 for a gala banquet and February 25 for the Twentieth Annual Mary Frances Early Lecture and Naming ceremony. I was scheduled to attend several additional gatherings.

On that Monday, I was picked up by a limo service along with Marilyn Holmes (wife of the late Hamilton Holmes) and my friend Minnie Haynes for the drive to Athens. Marilyn and I sat in the back seat and chatted a bit, but the lively chatter came from the front seat, which Minnie shared with the driver. I was nervous, excited, and wondered if I could get through the planned events without dissolving into an emotional state. The reality of having the College of Education named in my honor was so huge that I wondered if I could actually maintain my composure and just enjoy the momentous honor.

We arrived at the UGA Conference Center and hotel at 11:30 a.m. We checked into our individual rooms quickly. The annual GAPS (Graduate and Professional Scholars) luncheon was scheduled for 12:00 noon. Usually, this event was held on the evening preceding the lecture. This year, the event was planned for an earlier time because of the gala banquet that was to be held that evening. We were greeted by the GAPS students and ushered to a special table for me and my guests. I was surprised at the large number of students (approximately 50) who were there. I had thought that many of them would be unable to come because of the earlier time. After the meal, the students introduced themselves one by one and told us their home city/state and their majors. I always request this information because the composition of the group changes from year to year. Several proudly announced that they were receiving their doctorate degrees this year. I asked if any were experiencing any problems. No one responded to this usual question. I spoke to them briefly and asked Marilyn Holmes to share any words of wisdom. She told them that she was amazed with the wide variety of majors that they had described. At that point, I was presented an original painting of the College of Education with my name included, by Broderick Flanagan. This was a gift from him and the GAPS students. When I arrived at my room—a lovely suite—I noticed a beautiful vase of flowers that was from the Graduate School and the GAPS organization. I was thankful for both.

After the luncheon I was driven to the Athens home of Grady Thrasher and Kathy Prescott by my friend Nancy Butler. She was waiting for me when I left the luncheon. Nancy is always so helpful when I visit Athens. I had arranged the visit before I left home. Grady and Kathy are such wonderful friends and I rarely have the time to see and talk with them when I am in Athens. We were greeted warmly when we arrived. We went into their elegant sitting room and sat down to chat. Kathy brewed some Earl Grey tea and brought the tea and her famous pecan finger cookies for us to enjoy. It was so relaxing to just sit and talk with my friends. Nancy reminded me that we had to return to the hotel by 4:30 so that I could dress for the gala. Of course, Kathy and Grady would be in attendance but we all knew that we wouldn't see much of each other there.

Nancy and I returned to the hotel and she helped me to dress. I had chosen to wear a silver flutter-sleeve cocktail dress. My friend Donata came to arrange a matching swirl scarf. My cousin Patrice came to assist with my hair and makeup. We went downstairs for the reception that was outside the banquet room. I wandered through the crowd and hugged and shook hands with hundreds of friends, former students, and colleagues. I was soon whisked away to go into the venue where the banquet was being held. The room was decorated with sparkling white tablecloths and beautiful centerpieces. I was greeted at the head table by President Morehead. Dr. Michael F. Adams (UGA president emeritus) came to hug and greet me. The doors were opened and people streamed in to find their assigned tables. I was amazed at the crowd of over 500 that filled the room. After a sumptuous dinner that was served with great efficiency, the program began. Dominique Holloman served as mistress of ceremonies. I won't recount memories of the entire program but some highlights included a tribute to me by my former Coan Middle School student Lance Jackson. The crowd laughed when he said that he loved me more than bacon! The illustrious Michael Thurmond, native of Athens and CEO of DeKalb County, brought down the house with his remarks on "What ifs." This was truly a magical night. After taking several photos with friends and family, I decompressed with a ride around town with my good friend Vanessa Smith. Returning to my room after a very long day, I thought: "Those were Camelot moments." I slept well that night.

I woke early the next morning because I had planned an early morning breakfast at the home of another Athens friend, Joan Zitzelman.

Nancy picked me up at the hotel after purchasing local chicken biscuits and roasted potato tots. Joan supplied fruit and French-press coffee. We ate while enjoying talk about the previous evening and the upcoming main event for that day.

We couldn't linger over breakfast because I was to be taken to the College of Education building at 10:30 a.m. for a "First Look." I had not seen the building that now listed my name. A small crowd of family and Minnie's family—my extended family—were driven to the site. When we disembarked the van, my cousin Ray walked beside me. When I saw the building with "Mary Frances Early College of Education" emblazoned across the top, I was awe-struck. I fought to maintain my composure. This momentous honor tugged at my heart and my entire being! As we approached the doors leading into the building, several things caught my eye. A large Georgia bulldog stood with a sign that read "Welcome Ms. Early." A huge floor mat with the name of the building fronted the doors. The mat was black with white lettering. I said to no one in particular: "I can't walk on my name." When our small entourage entered the building, I was blinded by a phalanx of photographers who clicked away. I felt like a celebrity! The interior resembled a museum. Larger than life photos of me covered the walls with images from my youth through my days at UGA. Quotes from speeches that I had made over the years were printed over the photos. One photo included an interactive feature. If one placed a smartphone over that space, one could hear a segment of the commencement speech that I delivered in 2007. I couldn't help but shed some tears, but kept them to a minimum because of the photographers. Three beautifully arranged display cases held memorabilia from high school days, college, the University of Georgia, and my career. A plaque that was draped in black was prominently displayed for all to see after the naming ceremony. I was finally allowed to sit for a brief interview. I'm afraid that I was not at my best because this "First Look" was just too overwhelming for an eighty-three-year-old. We left the building and several photos were taken with administrators, my family, and extended family. We boarded the van for the trip back to the hotel. A special luncheon for invited guests was scheduled for noon. I had to hurry back to my room to get dressed for the day's main event.

I was so emotionally drained that dressing in my true red dress with black accoutrements was done in a fog. Luckily, I once again had friends and family to assist me. We went to the luncheon. Approximately 200 guests were in attendance. I was introduced to members of the Board of Regents and other important guests. Marilyn Holmes was seated at the head table with me, President Morehead, Marion Ross Fedrick, her husband, and others. I had invited Marilyn as my guest for the two days and wanted to spend as much time as possible with her. I looked around to see if my church friend Nancy Shealy was present. I had invited her and her caregiver, Tiffany Hutchins, to the luncheon and the Lecture/Naming ceremony. Nancy had been providing me with meals that were cooked by Tiffany. That wonderful gesture over time had allowed me to focus on my writing and the ongoing events. Though everyone was wearing name tags, I couldn't read them. When I mentioned this problem to President Morehead, he spoke to the coordinator of servers. One of them found Nancy and steered me to her table so that I could greet her. These and other acts of kindness proliferated throughout the three days in Athens. So many of my family and friends told me how friendly and helpful the entire host of UGA personnel had been throughout their stay.

Alton Standifer, the current assistant to the president, spoke to the luncheon guests about the upcoming event, including how they would be seated in reserved sections of the Performing Arts auditorium.

A van transported me and my family/guests to the Hodgson School of Music. The day was sunny, balmy, and perfectly beautiful for the historic event. When our van temporarily slowed to a halt because of the number of cars progressing to the event, a transportation coordinator who was riding in the van with us used her radio/walkie talkie to instruct the deck personnel to just let cars in without a pass inspection. She told someone that the traffic was clogged and that the program starting time was imminent. This done, our van progressed to a back entrance and we were ushered into the green room.

The first person who approached me was Governor Brian Kemp. He came to me with outstretched hand. His wife, Marty, came forward for a hug. Soon afterward, we were ushered to the front row of the auditorium.

Two of my former Coan students, Miranda Mack and her friend, ran down the steps to greet me. My family, a busload of Turner High alumni (approximately fifty), and a host of Alpha Kappa Alpha sorority sisters were also seated near the front, along with prominent guests.

The program began with a warm welcome from President Morehead. He then related the significance of the event. Introductions of the illustrious guests followed. He introduced me and when I stood and waved to the audience, I received thunderous applause.

Ashley Love, vice president of the Graduate and Professional Scholars (GAPS), introduced the keynote speaker. This organization holds the distinction of initiating the Mary Frances Early Lecture twenty years ago. The speaker, Marion Ross Fedrick, serves as president of Albany State University. She is also an alumna of the University of Georgia where she earned both bachelor's and master's degrees. This lecture was the first time that a UGA alumni has served in this role. President Fedrick delivered an impressive speech that centered on me and how I had made it possible for her and hundreds of others to attend UGA. She described me as a servant leader and urged members of the audience to counsel and encourage other students to ignore difficulties and to pursue their degrees.

After her speech President Morehead remarked on the initiative to name the College of Education in my honor and introduced Mr. Steve Wrigley, chancellor of the University System of Georgia. The chancellor's remarks brought tears to my eyes as he stressed the importance of music education to our nation. His remarks about his utter lack of musical ability elicited laughter from the audience. I felt humbled when he spoke about my contributions to UGA and the state of Georgia.

After the chancellor's remarks Dean Denise Spangler spoke about her pride in leading the Mary Frances Early College of Education. She told the audience that the fundraising initiative had resulted in over 900 donors who donated over $3 million to the endowment. This information brought loud applause from the audience and from me. She explained further that the funds would be used to make the Mary Frances Early professorship a distinguished position. She also said that the scholarship fund for GAPS outstanding students would be endowed. The remainder of the funds would be used for scholarships to deserving education and music education students.

Dr. Spangler then introduced Zoe Willingham, a twelfth-grader from Martha Stillwell High School in Clayton County. Zoe is also a participant in the Atlanta Symphony Orchestra's Talent Development Program, which I helped to found. And yes! we had to have music on this historic occasion. Zoe came onstage and performed the *Partita in E Major* by Johann Sebastian Bach. This unaccompanied violin solo was performed with passion, with impeccable intonation, and with nuanced dynamic levels. I had heard Zoe perform this very difficult composition at a recent Talent Development Program recital and had recommended her to participate in the day's program. Ryan Walks, coordinator of the TDP, and Zoe's mother accompanied her to Athens for the event. At the conclusion of this beautifully performed solo, the audience exploded in applause and a standing ovation. This young Black musician was a product of an orchestra program in a public school. She was also coached by one of the Atlanta Symphony Orchestra's violinists. She was accepted into the TDP by audition. Who says that public education cannot produce greatness?

Following this wonderful performance, President Morehead invited me, Governor Brian Kemp and his wife, Chancellor Wrigley, and Dean Denise Spangler to the stage. The big moment had arrived. President Morehead read a portion of the wording on the "Naming" plaque and came to the center to unveil it with my help. We unveiled the plaque very slowly to the applause of the audience. An official photo was taken and I proceeded to the microphone to make brief remarks.

Since I was seated in the front row of the auditorium, I had not seen the size of the audience. I don't have much central vision and could not see people at a distance. I could see, however, that the entire audience seemed full with people standing around the walls and in the balcony. I exclaimed at the large audience and its diversity. I said: "This is why I came." I recited the last portion of Robert Frost's poem "The Road Not Taken": "I shall be telling this with a sigh somewhere ages and ages hence: Two roads diverged in a wood, and I—I took the one less traveled by. And that has made all the difference." I explained that the road not taken would have been a return to the University of Michigan where I was enjoying my postgraduate studies. Instead I took the road less traveled—the road to the University of Georgia. I did this because I was compelled to play a role in integrating the UGA Graduate School and thus assist in the struggle of my fellow Turnerites, Charlayne and Hamilton. I said that in life we all make choices. I made the choice to help integrate UGA because it was the right thing to do at that time. I concluded my remarks by relating that the most wonderful words that I often heard were: "Thank you for paving the way." I thanked all those who had helped to plan and to implement the two days of honor—an honor that I could not have ever imagined.

Dr. Michelle Garfield Cook, provost for Diversity and Inclusion, closed the program with inspirational words. She invited the audience members to attend the reception that was being held in the lobby.

I was ushered back to the stage to take photos with groups and with individuals. Thankfully, a tall stool was placed at center stage close to the dedication plaque so that I could sit. I was so happy to see the Turner Alumni group, my Alpha Kappa Alpha sisters from Atlanta and the UGA chapter, my family and extended family group—and then seemingly hundreds of others who wanted to take a photo with me. It was heartwarming to see family and friends not only from all over the state of Georgia, but other states including Alabama, Florida, North and South Carolina, California, and Virginia. I was told later that over 1,000 people had attended this very historic event.

After an hour of taking photos, going to the green room to refresh with a cup of tea, and more photos onstage, the van drove my group back to the hotel. I was exhausted but still bubbling with joy at this most historic honor. I rested for a few minutes in my suite and then went to the Magnolia Room restaurant at the hotel for a parting dinner with my cousins, Nancy Butler, and Minnie. We enjoyed our wind-down time together with lively conversation, hugs and kisses. My cousins prepared to drive back to Monroe, metro Atlanta, and to Florida.

As I relaxed in my room, I relived the events over the past two days. I had asked Minnie to stay overnight and ride back in our limo on the next day. I sat in my room and relished the happy memories of the many Camelot moments I had experienced.

Though I cannot list all of the honors that I have received from UGA, one can readily see that I have been richly rewarded. After thirty years of not being known, much has happened since the year 2000. Reconciliation represents a wonderful state of being. My heart is now full of compassion for this institution and I enjoy being an ambassador of sorts, recruiting good students to come to UGA and encouraging those enrolled not to be daunted by the challenges the school and society place in front of them. Students today know they have a right (and an obligation?) to attend our state's flagship university and all schools and colleges under the aegis of the University System of Georgia. I take great satisfaction in knowing that I was a part of the struggle that made that happen.

After arriving home on Wednesday, I was inundated with congratulatory calls, cards, and emails. This continued throughout the entire week. On the next Saturday, I was driven back to Athens for another honor—this time from the Athens community. My longtime friend Cynthia Terry accompanied me to the annual Michael L. Thurmond Lecture series. This Black History program featured Dr. Maurice C. Daniels as keynote speaker. Held at the First A.M.E. Church, the program honored three hometown heroes and me. Dr. Daniels delivered an inspiring speech. I was awed, however, with a group of young children who delivered individual poems by black poets. Their performances were delivered with confidence and powerful inflections. Three of the children were as young as six years of age. Their performances were simply superb. Presentation of awards followed. I was so proud to be included with the three community leaders who are doing incredible work in the Athens area. A sumptuous reception followed the program. I was warmly greeted with hugs and words of congratulation. As Cynthia and I were driven home, I mused on the program and the brilliant performances by the children. I felt that if these young people continued on their path of excellence, Athens, UGA, and the entire nation would benefit from their contributions.

On the following Monday, I experienced another recognition that carried a sense of déjà vu. I was transported to the Georgia State Capitol to be recognized by the House of Representatives and the Georgia Senate. The House recognition was probably initiated by UGA alumna Dominique Holloman. Dominique serves as chief of staff for Representative William K. Boddie. A four-degree graduate of UGA, Ms. Holloman kept me informed regarding the delays and protocol for the visit. The two legislative bodies were forced to delay the event twice because of pressing issues that fell to both chambers.

As my cousin Patrice drove me and her mother, Sandra Kaye, to the Capitol, I thought about the newspaper article in 1961 when officials at the state capitol reluctantly decided that they had no choice but to admit me. Obviously, the officials in 2020 possessed different political views. What a contrast! They wanted to recognize me as the first African American to earn a degree from the University of Georgia as well as for the recent honor of the College of Education being named for me. After being told that I could invite only seven family or friends to accompany me for this honor, I carefully chose those whose schedules would allow them to attend this important occasion.

The first recognition was from the House of Representatives. Ms. Holloman met us after we cleared security and ushered us to a hallway where we sat until our appointed time. When we entered the House chamber, I was amazed at the large number of representatives who were seated in the room.

I was led to the stage with my seven family members and friends. Congressman William K. Boddie introduced me, read Resolution 967 with several "Whereas" commendations, and presented me with the printed resolution. I made brief remarks to them. The resolution with its thick cover emblazoned with a huge gold House seal is beautiful. It will be treasured forever as a symbol of my being recognized by the state of my birth.

After the ceremony, I took several photos with members of the House of Representatives. Dominique Holloman treated me and my guests to lunch at the nearby Sloppy Floyd cafeteria. We were impressed with Dominique's efficient planning on our behalf. I remembered how beautifully Dominique had served as mistress of ceremonies at the 2018 documentary. I remembered, too, how easily she presided at the gala program that preceded the naming ceremony, that she was a 40 Under 40 honoree for the UGA Alumni Association in 2017, and how hard she worked on the Black Alumni Board of Directors. I was so proud of this black alumna who earned one of her degrees from the College of Education. Now a major player in our state House of Representatives, she was forging a wonderful legacy of her own!

The Senate session was scheduled for that afternoon. This time, we were ushered into the Senate chamber to await our appointed time. After being seated on the front row of the room, I observed senators dashing about and talking with their colleagues. It was obvious that work was being done as there was great hubbub going on until the President of the Senate called the room to order.

The presentation of Senate Resolution 726 followed other business items. I was so happy that Senator Horacena Tate, daughter of the late Horace Tate, served as the presenter. Dr. Horace Tate was the initiator of the fund that made it possible for me to return to UGA for the spring and summer quarters in 1962. His daughter, Senator Horacena Tate, represents the 38th District of Georgia, the district in which I reside. I was so gratified to receive this distinctive honor as she introduced me and read the proclamation. The "Whereas" commendations were essentially the same as those of the House of Representatives. After receiving that impressive proclamation, I made brief remarks. When we were directed to the anteroom, many senators left the session to take photos with me. The two events gave me much satisfaction because I had received kudos from my state house and senate representatives. The implications of the outstanding honor from UGA in naming the College of Education in my name was continuing to bring tears to my eyes and joy to my soul.

The honors did not stop with the preceding events. On Monday of the next week, I was scheduled to receive an award from the Decatur City Commissioners, and on that Wednesday, I was to be recognized by DeKalb County's CEO Michael L. Thurmond as a Bridge Builder at the annual DeKalb County State of the County program. In response to the stern warnings of the spreading Covid virus pandemic, I had to make regrets to both organizations. Both were subsequently cancelled. Even so, I felt so richly rewarded to be recognized by the City of Decatur and DeKalb County where I lived. The decision to stay safely at home, however, did not blot out a wonderful feeling that my contributions were recognized across a broad spectrum of Georgia.

CHAPTER TEN

Coda: My Life Lessons

—————

My life has been richly blessed with an abundance of exhilarating, challenging, and rewarding pathways. As I reflect on my journey of eighty-three years, I marvel at the myriad life lessons that I have learned along the way. As an imperfect human being, I still make mistakes and fail to live up to those life lessons. But I try daily to listen to what my journey has taught. The roads I traveled have revealed a plethora of realities, not one single reality. Some are worth sharing.

Love of family, friends, colleagues, and even strangers represents the most important ingredient of life. I encourage everyone to nurture those relationships and you will never feel lonely or despondent.

From my birth through many years, I was surrounded, loved, and nurtured by many family members. Along the way, I accrued innumerable friends and colleagues with whom I enjoyed pleasant days. When I went to the University of Georgia, developing friendships was at first quite difficult. I persisted and some did reach out to me, particularly during my second degree. Family and friends at home remained my mainstay and support. After the reconciliation period, that group expanded exponentially. Today, with a rapidly advancing visual disability, I am blessed with cousins and friends who help me to live life fully. I am often approached by strangers who say that they are UGA graduates—and the circle of friends is increased. As a by-product, I have more lunch, dinner, and event invitations than I can manage. I lost two dear friends in 2018. I miss both of them each day. The first was Betty Williford, who was one of the few white graduate students to befriend me at UGA. After those years, we both worked as music teachers in the Atlanta Public Schools. When I moved to a supervisory position, Betty was one of our most talented music specialists. After we both retired, we often attended organ recitals and other music events together. We had lunch, most often at Sweet Tomatoes because we really enjoyed the soups and salads there. Betty was featured in the documentary *Mary Frances Early: The Quiet Trailblazer.*

The other friend was Joanne Lincoln with whom I traveled for over forty years. Joanne served as chief librarian at the Atlanta Public Schools Instructional Services Center. Our first trip together was to West Africa and then to Brazil. Many other travel adventures on every continent followed. After we retired from the school system, we attended the subscription series of the Atlanta Symphony Orchestra. We also had subscriptions to the Candler concert series at Emory's Swartz Center and attended the Woodruff Arts Museum at Emory's Carlos Museum. I have wonderful memories of times spent together with both of these friends. My advice is to hold fast to your family members and friends. One never knows when they will not be there to love and enjoy.

Don't be daunted by failure. It is a natural part of life and helps one to forge a path forward with wisdom.

Like most people, I have experienced many failures throughout my life and career. I have never, however, allowed those failures to defeat me. The most significant failure was my inability to find a husband. That was one of my dreams when I chose Clark College rather than an all-female institution. Though I was actually engaged to a fellow Clark-ite in my senior year, I returned the ring to him after my commencement. We were good friends and I enjoyed his company. I just didn't feel that I wanted to spend the remainder of my life with him. I wanted to begin my teaching career and go on to graduate school. I dated several men throughout my career, but never felt that any of them was the right one. Several, however, have remained lifelong friends.

"La belle vie" or the "good life" does not require a great deal of wealth. Though money is an essential for living, money alone does not guarantee true happiness. A career for which you have passion is far better than one that merely accrues wealth. When you find your true niche in life, pursue it with as much energy and passion as you possess.

If you have read the chapter on my career, you will agree that I did pursue my chosen area of music education with passion. I was aware that a career in music education would not result in earning a huge salary. It did, however, result in a joyful and satisfying life. So much has changed since my era of a single, lifetime career. Today, students may experience several career paths before finding the one that actually fits. I advise today's students to broaden their education rather than limit it to a single subject area. The ability to find a job for which one has a passion widens if one has expertise in more than one area.

Learn the art of patience. Good things do come to those who wait. You, however, have a role to play in making that happen. As Mahatma Gandhi reportedly said: "You must be the change you wish to see in the world."

I followed Mahatma Gandhi's mantra when I made the decision to help in the integration of the University of Georgia and become a civil rights activist. Though my role in this life-changing venture was forgotten for over thirty years, my pioneering efforts have now been recognized. This resulted in so many honors and recognitions that I could never have imagined. I just went on with my career and now realize that this was the plan fostered by God.

Don't be afraid to verbally challenge biased issues with which you disagree. Your views may not be accepted, but you won't feel like a hypocrite. Remember that silence means consent. Dr. Martin Luther King Jr. once said: "The time is always right to do what is right."

We can always disagree without becoming disagreeable. I remember once while working at Coan Middle School disagreeing with a request made by the principal who replaced Mr. Ralph Long. The principal told me that Coan was participating in a football game on the next Saturday, and that he wanted the band to march across the field while playing march music. I told him that our band would not be able to do this because our young music students were not developmentally ready to march while playing. I suggested that the band could play if they were seated. He said that the excitement of a marching band would generate more interest in the audience. I explained once again that this was not age-appropriate for our young students and that we just could not do that. He looked at me and said, "Your reply sounds like insubordination." The band did not participate in the football game and I didn't receive a letter of termination. I felt that I had to protect our students and stuck to my principles.

Embrace the joy of reading; that skill will prepare you for whatever you encounter. Traveling the world prepares you in the same manner.

From an early age, I read voraciously. I attribute this passion for reading to encouragement and modeling from my mother. As stated earlier, I read each day at the Auburn Avenue Branch Library and read at home. I also traveled broadly both internationally and in the United States. I learned so much through reading and traveling. My deepest regret now is that my impaired vision does not allow me to read printed materials. Though I have invested in several devices with magnification, they are not adequate to allow me to do what I dearly love to do. I solve that problem with the help of audiobooks.

Take care of your personal health. Excellent health allows one to enjoy a productive life.

In today's fast-food, fast-paced world, this has become more difficult. I have found that aging brings on its own health challenges—many that seem inevitable. But taking care of and responsibility for one's health remains an important component of one's happiness.

Don't forget to nurture your "roots" and "wings." Both will take you to unbelievable heights.

In my writing about my life I have referred often to the importance of following the teachings of my parents. I have tried to adhere to those words of wisdom. Each of us should do the same.

Be adventuresome. Each day offers a golden opportunity to repeat or learn something new and inspiring.

Taking on new challenges was something that I embraced early in my career. When asked to write the script for an audiovisual guitar method and an accompanying teacher's manual, I didn't know if I could do it, but I was eager to try. Treading upon this unfamiliar ground led to success. New adventures experienced during my travels include riding a tall camel in Tunisia, taking a ski lift up a mountain in Chile (though I have acrophobia, a fear of heights), riding in a subterranean vessel to view the Great Coral reef in Australia (though I suffer from claustrophobia), enjoying an outdoor swing as an octogenarian, and many other daring adventures.

Take pride in your heritage. Chronicle that history before it is completely lost.

This is one important area that I did not do. I did not question my father, or my one grandparent, my grandmother. The same is true of my aunts and uncles. I did talk with my mother during my adulthood, but not enough. Unlike today, children did not ask too many questions about their heritage during my childhood. This was not encouraged by adults. I advocate that today's youth ask questions and even tape-record conversations about their parents' and relatives' early life.

Give generously as you are able. Giving to those in need will pay big dividends to you in the future. Give "forward" when you've been the recipient of a good deed.

My experience with giving has resulted in my receiving more than I have given. Giving of your time, talent, and resources results in a sense of pure joy. Giving forward brings the same good feelings. The chapter about my travel to Columbus, Georgia, serves as one reminder. An elderly white gentleman came to my rescue when I had a flat tire while traveling to a music conference. I have never forgotten that wonderful act of kindness. Giving to others helps to make this a better world.

Learn to listen attentively to others' points of view. If you listen carefully, you will learn volumes.

At times we pretend that we are listening to another's point of view. We are actually not listening; we are thinking of our response. It seems that today political gurus talk over each other at the same time. This results in cacophony with no actual understanding occurring among the talkers. Nothing is resolved. We would do well to avoid this type of communication because it is fruitless.

Always remember that life is for living—active living! A sedentary life is dull and unrewarding.

This truism often refers to those of us who are elderly or senior citizens. Sitting in a rocking chair for the entire day while watching television represents the best way to become miserable. We all need human interaction and purposeful things to do. Volunteering at a hospital, a church, or a school brings about a life that is worth living. Most communities have a senior citizens center where the elderly can exercise, play board games, swim, have meals with others, or attend interesting events. Remember that retirement does not—*should* not—represent the end of life. My busy schedule is sometimes tiring—but it always brings me much happiness.

Always give thanks to God or whatever deity represents your belief. A daily "attitude of gratitude" will yield a happy and fulfilling life.

When we have problems—physical, mental, or situational—we tend to complain. We all have low points in our lives. That's being human. When, however, those feelings wash over us, we should think of all of the things for which we can be grateful. My visual disability sometimes makes me feel despondent. When I can't see the outlet into which I'm attempting to insert a plug, when I can't see the labels in the grocery store, when I have difficulty in seeing the keys on my computer keyboard—I could go on and on—I feel so frustrated. But I try each day to think of those things that I *can* do. I refuse to allow the doldrums to make me feel defeated. Listening to inspiring music, calling someone to just chat, or listening to my latest book on my Echo, these things make me feel better. Sometimes, I type a listing of things for which I am grateful and instantly feel better.

When you feel that you have been wounded or hurt by another's actions— forgive. Don't spend fruitless time in attempting to retaliate. This is best left to a higher being. Forgiveness brings about the peace of mind that makes life worth living.

Forgiveness represents a gift to one's self. The fact that I was erased from UGA's history really hurt me for several years. I made a decision to forgive those who chose to do this; I forgave them and went on with my life. It is so rewarding to get rid of this type of burden from our consciousness. My spiritual community and faith in God made this possible. And reconciliation happened in a wonderful way.

Johnnetta Cole (the 2016 MFE guest lecturer at UGA) says that we should all write our stories. Doing this is cathartic and will reveal one's true self. Just do it before you are an octogenarian like me!

Writing this memoir was truly a challenge for me—but I am so happy that I did it. I encourage each of my readers to do the same.

These aphorisms are not intended as a roadmap for the reader. They represent *my* truths. Yours may be different but I hope you will take the time to reflect and get yours down on paper or shared with someone you love.

I am grateful in so many ways for the life I have led. From the naïve but curious child raised in the South during wartime and Jim Crow, to the halls of academe and beyond, my experience has been a beautiful, if complex, symphony. In so many ways, music was the guide; it also brought me solace and inspiration as an educator and administrator. I trust you, too, will listen for the music that will shepherd you on your own journey.

Appendix:
Diary Excerpts

These excerpts from my diary were printed in the *Atlanta Inquirer* on Saturday, June 24, 1961:

Snubs, Loneliness, Friends, a Birthday Surprise . . .

Jottings from My U. of Ga. Diary

(Miss Early, John Hope School faculty member and a member of the staff of the *Atlanta Inquirer*, has agreed to share informally with our readers some of her experiences and thoughts as the first Negro graduate student to enroll at the University of Georgia.)

By Mary Frances Early

MONDAY

Uneventful trip down—or too sleepy to note the difference! Reason? Retired the night before at 1:30, arose at 5:00. . . .

Arrived in Athens at approximately 7:45. Went directly to Dr. Kelly's office, met by Nell Hudson, his secretary. Learned that I had received two calls—one from Rev. King of Westminster House, the other from May March with whom I was to register. Contacted Miss March. She suggested that we wait until about 10:30 before trying to register because lines would be much too long. Sat down to wait it out. . . .

A young law student came into the office to welcome me to the Classic City. We had interesting chat. He is not in summer school but is training to go to Pittsburgh to sell fruitcakes. Tall, easy-going fellow. Good conversationalist. After talking for a while we decided to go to Mrs. Killian's Restaurant for breakfast. We went in my friend B. Wayne's car and as we all climbed into the front seat the young man drew curious stares from some observers of his own hue. Incidentally, he's a native Georgian from down near Waycross.

Breakfast was delicious and was over all too soon. We returned to the office just before May March drove up. May and I hopped into her car and started for the campus. I felt very much at ease because we immediately liked each other and chatted about ourselves on the way. May is from North Carolina, has an amusing soft, Southern drawl and is, in short, a delightful person. She is a graduate student in Art.

We stopped in the Fine Arts Building, where both of us would have classes, for her catalog. She introduced me to a fellow student of hers from Germany. He had a charming accent but spoke English exceptionally well. We met him on the stairway and we were standing on the steps conversing when a white woman and her little boy came up the steps toward us. We moved aside so that she'd have room to pass but when she approached me she turned beet red and sidled past—so that she wouldn't touch the brown dye, I suppose!

May and I went on over to Stegman and were horrified to find that the line was still ten miles long. As we came down the steps to the line it seemed that every head turned our way, but we continued walking to the end. The line moved into the building very rapidly and once we got inside we were sorry we had, for it appeared that we had stumbled into complete chaos. Though there seemed to be no system, actually there was. Once again—stares, stares, stares. May and I had to separate because we were in different fields and I got rather shaky because I didn't think I'd ever really get through all those endless lines. The faculty members who assisted with registration were exceedingly kind and helpful. I saw Mr. Danner, the Registrar, standing beside the wall, rocking back and forth on his heels with his arms folded, calmly surveying the seeming confusion.

After about two hours we completed the first portion of our registration. We then moved to the Academic building to pay our fees. I was very glad to get out of that steaming gymnasium because it was so hot, that I thought I'd pass out.

When we reached the Academic building May found that she had to go to the bank so I went in alone. I went up to the Dean of Women's office to get my housing assignment. There was not a card made out for me so I had to wait until one was made. I couldn't help wondering if someone had doubted that I was actually coming. . . .

After paying fees I breathed a sigh of relief and walked back to Dr. Kelly's office, since it was closer than May's car. Through it all, I was practically unnoticed.

B. Wayne and I left the office and went to Center Myers dormitory where I was to lie. He carried my luggage into my room after we had met the housemother, Mrs. Porter. I guess by then I was looking a little droopy because she warned me that I would need a fan—and I did!

This was my first summer in Georgia for six years, and I had forgotten how hot it could get.

After unloading all of my baggage, we went to the Colonial store for some food supplies. When we returned I (a bit sadly) bid B. Wayne adieu. I stood at the window and watched as he passed by on the way back to Beautiful Atlanta. At that moment a well of loneliness began yawning inside me, so I started wearily to unpack. . . .

When I finally finished it was 5:30 p.m. I was to have called Dr. Kelly at 6 to arrange to have dinner, but I made the mistake of lying across the bed to rest my truly weary bones for a second. I was so exhausted that I slept until 8:30 and had to make sandwiches instead. As I ate, I viewed my little suite with delight and decided—"God's in His Heaven, All's right in the world!"

So ended my first day at the University of Georgia.

TUESDAY

Arose at 7 a.m. and prepared breakfast (coffee and cereal), readied myself for class. My first class was at ten and lasted for two hours. I didn't know if I could stand Advanced Music History for that long! Found that I could.

Came back to the dorm and prepared lunch (sandwich and Coke). As I ate, I reflected upon the attitude of students I'd met. Most of them simply ignored me. Mr. Mitchell, our instructor, was interesting, though he smoked a pungent old pipe throughout his lecture. Our class was small—most graduate music classes are. We got a heavy assignment right off the bat—to read a philosophical article about Aristoxenus, Greek musician and philosopher.

I found that I was tired after walking to and from class. Distance plus hills = weariness. . . . I trudged back up the hill again to my 1:30 class, which I couldn't find because the meeting place had been changed. I was frantic. I didn't want to be late. I went into the music library and Mrs. Dunaway, the librarian, came up, introduced herself and greeted me warmly. When I asked her help in locating my Advanced Theory class she very graciously complied.

When the class was over I was thoroughly convinced that I had selected the most difficult offered. The instructor, Mr. John Anderson, was a small, jolly fellow who seemed packed with knowledge and theory.

My last class—Vocal Problems—was taught by a Mr. Leonard. He speaks with a Germanic accent, has the airs of a singer and talks as though he may be a tough customer to please. Of my three instructors he seemed to appreciate my presence least.

I stopped at the library after class to begin work on Grecian music and found it to be hard going. I think I could understand the Greek better than I understood the English translation!

One of my classmates, a Swedish woman, invited me to go to the bookstore with her. This I did, as I had some purchases to make also. After purchasing books and supplies I went back to the library. The grind had really begun. . . . A fellow in my M.H. class sat down at the table and talked for a while. He, too, was having trouble comprehending the Greek article.

Back to the dorm, dressed for dinner at Killian's with Dr. Kelly. I was treated to filet mignon. Studied late. Then to bed.

WEDNESDAY

Arose at 7 and, wondering why my bones creaked so, I remembered that this day was my 25th birthday. (P.S.: I won't have any more.)

The day went along very uneventfully. I began, however, to feel a bit lonely, what with being snubbed by most of the students and having to do everything alone.

I still had not eaten in the dining hall because I was hoping to strike up an acquaintance with someone from my dorm with whom I could dine. I had a few qualms about going to the dining hall and eating alone. I was feeling more and more depressed and downhearted. Then I got a phone call. It was May March, inviting me to have "hot dogs" at the Westminster House.

I bathed, dressed and was picked up by Dr. Popovitch, professor of Speech, who had written to me before I came to Athens. He was a very gentlemanly escort and made me feel quite at ease on our way up. At the House I met Rev. and Mrs. Corky King—a very young and delightful couple who have two darling baby girls—Mary Scott and Margaret. One of my M.H. classmates, John, a Greek, and his girl friend, Donna, were there also—along with May March. We had an outdoor picnic with charcoal broiled hamburgers, relishes, and baked beans.

It was so good to have some people to eat and talk with. I was simply flabbergasted when Mary Lyle (Mrs. King) came out with a beautiful birthday cake with one lighted candle! ... They all sang "Happy Birthday" as I made a wish and I could scarcely keep the tears back as I thought of how these wonderful people, who didn't even know me, could remember my birthday!

Of course, we had ice cream to top it off. It began to rain so we went into the house and talked. It got late and as much as I hated to have the evening end, I remembered the work awaiting me at the dorm.

Dr. Popovitch, who had furnished the cake and ice cream, took me on a short tour of the campus on the way home. He told me about the Wednesday night riot in January outside Charlayne's suite—the same quarters I am occupying. Dr. Popovitch discussed the integration problem quite frankly and as we walked into the dorm he told me that I could feel free to ask his help on any problems I might have this summer.

He expressed his desire that I might stay on for the fall session. He spoke very warmly of Charlayne. I signed in, gave Mrs. Porter a piece of my cake and said goodnight. So ended my 25th birthday—one I'm sure I'll never forget!

Selected Bibliography

BOOKS AND FILMS

Daniels, Maurice, Senior Researcher and Executive Producer. *Foot Soldier for Equal Justice: Horace T. Ward and the Struggle to Enter the University of Georgia* (film). UGA's Foot Soldier Project for Civil Rights Studies in conjunction with the Richard B. Russell Library for Political Research and Studies and the Office of Instructional Support and Development, 2001.

Daniels, Maurice, Senior Researcher and Executive Producer. *Mary Frances Early: The Quiet Trailblazer* (film). UGA's Foot Soldier Project for Civil Rights Studies in conjunction with the Richard B. Russell Library for Political Research and Studies and the Office of Instructional Support and Development, 2018.

Ecke, Melvin W. *From Ivy Street to Kennedy Center: A Centennial History of the Atlanta Public School System*. Atlanta: Atlanta Board of Education, 1972.

Green, Victor Hugo. *The Negro Motorist Green Book*. New York, 1936.

McConathy, Osbourne. *The Music Hour*. Boston: Silver-Burdette, 1929.

McCoo, Edward P. *Ethiopia at the Bar of Justice*. In *Plays and Pageants from the Life of the Negro*, edited by Willis Richardson. The Associated Publishers, 1930.

Shipp, Bill. *Murder at the Broad River Bridge: The Slaying of Lemuel Penn by the Ku Klux Klan*. Atlanta: Peachtree Publishers, 1981.

Thrasher, Grady, and Kathy Prescott. *Athens in Our Lifetime: Recalling the Evolution of Our Town over the Past Six Decades* (film). Watkinsville: Surprisingly Professional Productions, 2017.

Trillin, Calvin. *An Education in Georgia: Charlayne Hunter, Hamilton Holmes and the Integration of the University of Georgia*. Athens, GA: University of Georgia Press, 1964.

NEWSPAPER ARTICLES

Emerson, Bo. "1st Grad's Feat Little Known at UGA: As First Black Students Sparked Protests, She Quietly Earned Degree." *Atlanta Journal-Constitution*, May 9, 2013.

Powledge, Fred. "1ˢᵗ Athens Degree Awarded to Negro." *Atlanta Journal,* September 26, 1962.

Shannon, Margaret. "Georgia Accepts Negro: Graduate School to Admit Woman; Decision Due Soon on 13 for Tech," *Atlanta Journal,* May 10, 1961.

PERSONAL ITEMS FROM THE
MARY FRANCES EARLY COLLECTION IN
THE UGA SPECIAL COLLECTIONS LIBRARIES

Early, Mary Frances. Application letter to the University of Georgia, 1961. Mary Frances Early papers. Richard B. Russell Library for Political Research and Studies; Box 3; folder 1.

Early, Mary Frances. Entry in handwritten journal begun the first day of college at Clark College, 1953. Mary Frances Early papers. Richard B. Russell Library for Political Research and Studies; Box 4; folder 18.

King, Martin Luther, Jr. Letter from Dr. Martin Luther King Jr. to Mary Frances Early, 1962. Mary Frances Early papers, University of Georgia Archives (Hargrett Library); Box 1; folder 4.

University of Georgia student proclamation, 1961. "Students for Passive Resistance." Mary Frances Early papers, Richard B. Russell Library for Political Research and Studies; Box 3, folder 14